The Managemei

Studies in Teaching and Learning
General Editor
Denis Lawton, B.A., Ph.D.
Professor of Education and Director,
University of London Institute of Education

In the series:

The Management of Learning in the Classroom

Marten Shipman

HODDER AND STOUGHTON
LONDON SYDNEY AUCKLAND TORONTO

British Library Cataloguing in Publication Data

Shipman, M. D.
  The management of learning in the classroom.—
  (Studies in teaching and learning.)
  1. Learning   2. Educational psychology
  I. Title   II. Series
  370.15′23   LB1060

ISBN 0 340 34191 2

First published 1985

Printed and bound in Great Britain for
Hodder and Stoughton Educational,
a division of Hodder and Stoughton Ltd,
Mill Road, Dunton Green, Sevenoaks, Kent,
by Richard Clay (The Chaucer Press) Ltd, Bungay, Suffolk.
Typeset in 11/12 point Plantin by
Macmillan India Ltd, Bangalore-25

Contents

Studies in Teaching and Learning

The purpose of this series of short books on education is to make available readable, up-to-date views on educational issues and controversies. Its aim will be to provide teachers and students (and perhaps parents and governors) with a series of books which will introduce those educational topics which any intelligent and professional educationist ought to be familiar with. One of the criticisms levelled against 'teacher-education' is that there is so little agreement about what ground should be covered in courses at various levels; one assumption behind this series of texts is that there is a common core of knowledge and skills that all teachers need to be aware of, and the series is designed to map out this territory.

Although the major intention of the series is to provide general coverage, each volume will consist of more than a review of the relevant literature; the individual authors will be encouraged to give their own personal interpretation of the field and the way it is developing.

Introduction

Here is yet another attempt to use evidence from the human sciences to inform teachers and student teachers. In this case the focus is on the way learning is managed in the classroom. That smacks of the factory and the office. Yet all teachers are in the management business whether organising resources or acting as a resource. Where the emphasis is on the spontaneous, on individual initiative, on informality, this organisation becomes more, not less, important. This is why the evidence and the examples are from studies of primary schooling, for it is often there that the teacher as manager of learning can be seen at his/her most effective and most exciting. But the application of that evidence and its critical interpretation is important for secondary as well as primary schooling.

Behind this approach lies the optimistic assumption that teachers can boost the quality and quantity of learning among children in the classroom. Optimistic because much of the evidence from the human sciences has suggested that the dominant factors accounting for learning lie outside the control of teachers. If intelligence was innate or fixed at an early age, or attainment determined by social background, little could be done inside the school where both genetic and social engineering are not expected of teachers. But this optimism is not just based on observations of unflagging faith and effort in classrooms, but on the recent retreat of determinist thinking within the human sciences. Indeed, it was the coming together of the hopes expressed in staffrooms with those behind recent research in psychology and sociology that persuaded me to write yet another 'tips for teachers'. But no embarrassment should be necessary. There has been increasing investment in the human sciences over a hundred years and they should be contributing to making learning more effective.

The book rests on three sources of evidence. First, there is the mainly psychological evidence on learning in all its bewildering variety. Second, there is sociological evidence, often contradictory, but always closely concerned with the relevant factors inside and outside the school. Third, there are the studies of learning in the classroom. This research has produced a growing body of evidence on what goes on between teachers and children in the bustle of the school day.

This research evidence has been used as a basis for suggestions for improving the management of learning in classrooms. But the extraction of evidence and its interpretation for making recommendations has to be viewed as suspicious behaviour. My views, my examples, are unlikely to coincide with other attempts to underpin recommendations with evidence. Thus the book contains an opening chapter on the nature of human scientific research and the problems in interpreting evidence. That is not just a reflection of my own scepticism. It is intended to show the reader how such evidence can be judged as a dependable base for action. There has been a liberation within the different human sciences that has placed thinking humanity in the spotlight, replacing the conditioned, over-socialised being that made up the statistics in much pre-1970s empiricist psychology and sociology. But the acceptance that this change of model of humanity is liberating, the rejection of the fatalism, the hopelessness of the earlier model, and the optimism that this switch has produced a more useful and more valid body of evidence for reflecting on teaching, also bring a responsibility to spell out the weaknesses as well as the strengths of the research involved.

This profit and loss account of the research that informs practice in education is an invitation to treat psychology and sociology not as necessarily authoritative sources, but as another piece of evidence to add to everyday professional judgements. No doctor relies on a thermometer or a urine test alone. Professional experience and second opinions are the basis of diagnosis. So are they in teaching. The evidence from the research provides a source to aid that professional judgement. The medical comparison is appropriate. In the end, the effective management of learning in the classroom is about the diagnosis of the task in hand and of the knowledge, attitudes and skills of the children about to undertake it. Teachers are in the best position to analyse both. This book is an aid to that analysis.

1 The Assumptions behind the Evidence

This book is a celebration of the way individuals persistently become exceptions to laws put forward to explain their behaviour. Most books on the psychology or sociology of education present the factors which constrain individual behaviour, whether these are defined in terms of motivation, learning, personality within one subject, or of social norms and interactions in the other. The emphasis is on the patterns of behaviour that suggest predictability. Increasingly, however, the evidence from psychological and sociological research is of the resilience, the initiative, the interpretations of individuals as they make sense of and act to control social situations in and out of school. This facility for interpretation makes it unlikely that laws governing human activity will ever be found.

The sceptical approach to theories, to evidence, and to the consequent practices recommended because they are scientific, is not just a precaution when studying the use of the human sciences as a guide to learning and teaching. When I was a child, a doctor in Muswell Hill removed my tonsils, appendix, adenoids and foreskin, not because they were troublesome, but as the recommended preventative medical practice. Similarly, a dentist pulled my molar teeth just in case. My mother removed me to Finchley and younger practitioners before any more of the bits and pieces I have since found most useful were cut according to the best of current practice. Scepticism is advisable because the appeal to science gives an authority to professional practice that can be left intact for years after the scientists themselves have rejected the evidence they earlier promulgated as incontrovertible.

What Weight should be Placed on Evidence from the Human Sciences?

I have a few vague and muddled memories of my professional training as a teacher. I remember a list of instincts produced by McDougall that were supposed to provide the drive behind human action, a lecturer acting a life-like description of some pigeons taught to strut in a figure of eight, a film of some chimpanzees trying to reach bananas outside their cage and, above all, a photograph of a dog so frustrated that it rolled, comatose, on to its back, like Snoopy with rigor mortis. I was taught that intelligence was innate, accurately measurable, fixed early in life and difficult to alter. Children who were culturally deprived and who came from poor social backgrounds needed special help, but there was no evidence that any of it helped. In retrospect it seems utterly pessimistic.

There is usually a blend of science and folklore in the advice given to teachers. It is often difficult to distinguish them. Here, for example, are two laws of potential use to teachers:

1   *Yerkes-Dodson Law*   As the difficulty of tasks increases, the optimum motivation for learning or performance decreases.
2   *Murphy's Law*   If something can go wrong, it will.

The first of these is derived from the work of two psychologists, Yerkes and Dodson in 1908, working with rats. They noticed that the success rate for difficult tasks decreases more rapidly than that for easy tasks. The conclusions for teachers seem plain. A little tension may bring a useful motivation into children's work.

The second of these laws is not scientific in being the result of experimentation on rats, although it may rest on some canny observation of human behaviour. It may be used to give very useful advice to teachers in the same area of motivation as the Yerkes-Dodson Law. In a classroom you won't win all the time. Be prepared for the worst because it is sure to happen sometime.

What then is the basis for distinguishing one law as scientific from the other as rubbish? Certainly it is not to be found in the facts that only support Yerkes-Dodson. Writers can always find evidence to support their case. This is usually described as 'exampling', boosting an argument by selecting the facts that fit. Neither is scientific status based on the theories that explain the facts. From Murphy's stable there is Finagle's Law, 'No matter what occurs, there is always someone who believes it happened according to his pet theory' (*Omni*, 1979). This is why it is misleading to say that research in the human sciences 'proves' something. Human science could not stand up to Popper's view that what matters in science is not verification but falsification, the attempt to find a negative case that necessitates the rejection of the theory concerned (Popper, 1959). There are always cases that don't fit because humans are diverse, complex and contrary. On this criterion laws of human behaviour are unlikely. That is a hopeful conclusion. It means that no case is pre-determined; something can always be done.

How then does evidence come to be accepted as reliable and valid, and consequently suitable for use in advising teachers? As in all sciences, the final judgement is based on agreement among those who are in a position to give expert, authoritative verdicts. Thus it is the agreement among psychologists or among sociologists and so on that ultimately decides whether evidence is acceptable. To appreciate why this is possible and how it is organised, scientific disciplines have to be seen as communities similar to religious orders. They have seniors in positions of authority, those who are establishing a place and those hoping to join. Membership is secured through examination and apprenticeship. Promotion and recognition comes from publication, from delivering papers at conferences, or through taking a seminar and defending a thesis. Articles are refereed and the journals edited by professors and other senior members who also control promotion and act as external examiners. Their opinions decide the evidence that merits publication or communication at conferences, just as they decide who is appointed, made a senior lecturer, reader or professor. These scientific communities wherein evidence is judged are also cultures within which some activity comes to be accepted as normal.[1]

A group of ethogenic psychologists or social phenomenological sociologists have their own language, their own concepts for categorising as well as their own exclusive title.[2] They write for each other, meet at conferences, have their great and good, probationers and students. Evidence has to meet criteria laid down within often tight-knit communities and imposed through hierarchically organised authority. There is often a small closed circle, a fellowship who write for each other and spark off ideas together. But the values in these communities, the problems which are their concern, the language used and the judgements made about the relevance, reliability and validity of evidence are not necessarily those of teachers, of others in the education service or of human scientists whose allegiance is to another community. The language might be alien, the context unfamiliar, the judgement of evidence idiosyncratic when viewed from the classroom or town and county hall, or from an unorthodox position. Furthermore, academics tend to reward the innovator, the radical, the pioneer, rather than those who confirm, replicate and consolidate the activities that produce the dependable base that is sought by teachers, administrators and politicians.

Why is there so much Change in the Human Sciences and so much Contemporary Dispute?

The early adoption of the methods of the natural sciences to study human behaviour is of fundamental importance in understanding the limits on the use of the human sciences to guide practice in a subject such as education. This arises from the strengths and weaknesses of the method itself and the search for laws of human behaviour through the use of research designs developed in the natural sciences. Positivism contrasts with idealism in recognising only observable facts and experience as the source of reliable knowledge. Another term in frequent use to describe this approach is empiricism, where scientific laws are formulated on the basis of observation and experiment. Here it is the observed facts, often reduced to numbers, that count as knowledge. A version of this is behaviourism where the concern is with human action as a response to stimuli, not as the result of thinking things out. The common factor in these three definitions is a belief in collecting facts through observation, surveying, questioning, or experimentation.

The adoption of this method of studying human behaviour was motivated by the hope that there would be a pay-off in the study of human behaviour that would be equivalent to that in the natural sciences. Yet, in retrospect, the dangers were obvious. It was not just that human beings, fortunately, are not machines and that there are limits on how you can control them for experimentation. There was an assumption that had even more profound effects. Once social facts are seen as entities existing in the real world separate from the mind of the person observing or experimenting, they have no will of their own. They are governed by laws. The human beings observed lose their humanity. They become facts, data, statistics. Adopting this scientific method eliminated consideration of what was going on in the mind. The ability of humans to interpret and hence influence situations was ignored.

The consequences of this can be seen most clearly in the differences between two typical experiments used to collect evidence for use in education. The first uses rats. These are left until hungry and then placed in a maze. They learn to work through it to the food at the end. The evidence on the effects of increasing the hunger, or manipulating the difficulty of the twists, turns and barriers can be generalised to laws about learning applicable to humans. But humans placed in a maze have more options. They might attack the researcher, sleep through the experiment, or treat their hunger as a slimming cure. In conditions of severe stress they can alter their behaviour dramatically. More important, when humans are surveyed, asked questions, observed as they learn or teach, they are interacting with the researcher. They are acting intentionally, giving meaning to the situation, working it out. So is the researcher. There is no separation of subject and object.

Why is there such an Emphasis on Models in the Human Sciences?

The legacy of attempts to produce scientific models that could be used to explain human behaviour remains powerful. We have only just abandoned the idea that human behaviour sprang from instincts provided through natural selection. Teachers of my inter-war generation were trained using Nunn's *Education, its Data and First Principles* (1920) that incorporated these Darwinian views promulgated by McDougall in *An Introduction to Social Psychology* (first published 1908, 28th edition, 1946). We were also trained to be aware of the subterranean forces that limited individual rationality and of Freud's view that everybody needed continuing psychoanalysis. Marxism, with its emphasis on the inevitability of class struggle and of the false consciousness of those who do not see their part in it, remains a powerful contemporary influence. They are all deterministic, showing why humans had to behave that way, according to laws, or instincts or historical forces beyond their control. Yet one after another these models have been torpedoed. We are not necessarily what history, or evolution, or infantile experience make us. These may contain important influences, but the direction of evidence in the human sciences is away from inevitability and pre-determination towards the construction and re-construction of reality by active and aware humans. That is an optimistic message, even if it removes the certainty of early human science and places the responsibility for improving the human lot firmly on the parents, teachers and others as they educate. When human behaviour was seen as determined by historical, evolutionary or subconscious forces beyond the individual, inaction could be excused by reference to the inevitability of class oppression, the innate, unchangeable nature of intelligence or the need for psychoanalysis to uncover the roots of deviant behaviour. Removing the determinism is liberating. But it also increases the responsibility on those who can promote individual fulfilment.

By the 1960s there were strong counter-attacks on the elimination of common-sense explanations as a focus of study and of the tendency to use questionnaires or experimental stimuli to fit human responses into pre-determined categories in order to produce objective, quantitative data. In sociology, with an increased emphasis on interpretation, the focus swung to the way people experienced and created their own reality. In psychology, there was a similar attempt to treat humans as consciously acting to control their own lives and actively to process information. These new approaches aimed to put common sense back in the picture. Reports were often in everyday language. It was bottom-up rather than top-down human science. (For the sociological position, see Filmer, Silverman and Walsh, 1972; for the psychological position, see Harré and Secord, 1972.)

The interpretative sociologists and psychologists objected to the mechanistic model of man that was built into the adoption of scientistic methods in the study of humanity. The search for laws and the hope of predictability were seen as de-humanising the people being studied. Similarly, the theoretical level of analysis tended to change. Instead of looking to evolution, to an unrolling philosophy of history, at the repeating influence of human myths and complexes, the focus switched to the way individuals were making sense of their own world. The switch was particularly important in education. The rejection of the idea that it was necessary for experts to uncover the ulterior motives behind behaviour was especially significant for teachers who every minute of the day have to guess at the reasons for the behaviour in front of them. They have to assume that they do understand and are able to act to help or control. The insistence on a scientific explanation of behaviour suggested a degree of amateurism in the classroom that was insulting.

Human scientists share with us all the problem of the complexity of human behaviour. They solve it in the same way, by building models that simplify the factors involved. Just as coloured ping-pong balls can be wired together to model complicated molecules and hence help explain chemical reactions, so models of social groups or of learning can be constructed from concepts. They serve as a source for hypotheses or hunches about human behaviour that can be investigated, or can serve to explain the accounts given by those studied or observations made. The key to understanding evidence is the detection of the models used by those producing it, whether as the source for designing the research, or as the means of interpreting the accounts produced.

The problem with models is, firstly, that they may be confused with reality. Intelligence is seen as lodging somewhere in the brain rather than being inferred from behaviour. Society may be seen as an organism and policies formulated on that basis. Instincts are assumed to drive us to behave, rather than being explanations of behaviour thought up by psychologists. The second problem arises from the way models are constructed. They may be maps, equations, diagrams, physical constructions, or just collections of ideas that serve to understand complicated reality. Often they are analogies. We say that human societies are like an organism that has interrelated parts. We talk of the body politic, social structures, general will, group minds or collective consciences. We look to machines, to feedback loops, to telecommunications for ways of interpreting human thought. These analogies may help us to understand, yet can, at the same time, mislead. Societies may have some organic characteristics but they do not die or reproduce. Analogies don't fit or there would be no need for them. That flow chart is only a grossly simplified abstraction as a model for the human brain. There are rarely one or two factor explanations of human behaviour. Machines and systems as models for human relations or the mind can mislead. One position is to view society, or organisations such as schools, or the human mind, as organisms. With this view, obscured behaviour is interpreted by reference to the organic model, so that the parts observed are seen to contribute to the whole system, much as the kidneys or the white blood corpuscles serve the human body.

The third problem with many models is that they either mystify or reduce the complexity of human behaviour. Human scientists have started at two extremes in the modelling business. One position is to envisage society or the mind as a whole. Observed behaviour is referred to a comprehensive model, usually organic, so that the parts are seen to contribute to the whole, much as the kidneys serve the body or the carburettor the car engine. The problem here is that met in all analogies. The social relations, or the mind, become entities to which all else is referred. But the model is itself only an abstraction. The opposite approach is as misleading. Here the behaviour is dealt with in discrete parts. Stimulus-response bonds are hypothesised from observing simple responses to artificial stimuli. The richness of human interactions is reduced to an observation schedule and a series of ticks. At one extreme we mystify by analysing in terms of insights or functions and talking of false consciousness or the common good. At the other extreme, we devalue the richness of humanity by describing it in terms of reflexes, conditioned responses or computer algorithms.

This discussion of the use of models and theories also applies to concepts. When we classify observed behaviour as alienated or learning as insight, we are gathering together characteristics that are likely to arise from numerous historical and contemporary influences on each individual scrutinised. We only need concepts, theories and models when the facts we have seem a problem. We go to our models to interpret the data, whether we are human scientists using defined, public models or lay humans referring to our ill-defined and often forgotten 'models in the mind'. But reader, be cautious. It is a complicated issue and I have just used a model to explain the use of models. It seems to be in there. It helps me think through things I see as problematic. But I can't see it, assess its validity, its consistency, its relevance. As a human scientist I try to make some models public, give them definition, so that others may assess their credibility.[3] But even if there is unanimity over the model of intelligence, of learning, of culture or of social class, it is not likely to last long and a more usual state in the human sciences is for several models to conflict and compete.

How have Changes in Models of Human Science Research affected Advice on Teaching?

Psychologists, sociologists and other human scientists try to explain behaviour and relationships. They do this by formulating theoretical models of behaviour or social interaction from which explanations can be derived, hypotheses tested and abstractions checked against the concrete. Behind the recommendations that learning should be organised this way, or that classrooms should be laid out that way, are models of learning, of motivation, of interaction and so on. It has already been suggested that these models change rapidly. How then has the rejection of the positivist version of science that started by the end of the nineteenth century, and is still continuing, influence the kinds of evidence favoured in advice to teachers?

The first clue has already been given. At any particular time there will be popular, approved approaches within the human sciences. Faculty psychology dominated the nineteenth century development of the subject and was used to support the training of the powers of the mind in schools. It was replaced by psychology that emphasised biological and genetic factors. That led to a stress within education on individual differences. Some of the conclusions now seem not only unsupportable, but racist, sexist and elitist. The textbooks of one generation tend all to be written or at least influenced from limited points of view. If the genetic and instinctual bases of human behaviour of the 1950s were promulgated today they would be condemned as racist. Perhaps today's human science will be seen as absurd or objectionable tomorrow. Yet it forms the contemporary context for advising teachers.

There are losses as well as gains in development and it would be absurd to suggest that we are entering the golden age of human science as it guides educational practice. The effect has been to align the interests of teachers and researchers. This has occurred because the shift from behaviourism, positivism, empiricism, scientism has allowed attention to be focused on factors which have always been of major concern to teachers, not only because of their importance for helping children, but because they are possible to manage. The changed emphasis in the human sciences has increased both their scope and their hope for teachers and others responsible for children.

To be useful to teachers, evidence has to be related to matters that are under their control. It is only possible to act beneficially if recommendations are feasible, teachable, manageable. If human behaviour is driven by unconscious motives, is determined by evolution or is swept along by history unfolding according to dialectic materialism, teachers may justifiably feel that there is little they can do about little Fred's obstinacy or greed. If human learning is a matter of conditioning, then teaching can be reduced to routines aimed at delivering appropriate stimuli in the correct sequence. If intelligence is fixed at birth or formed by the age of five, teachers are clearly doing a hopeless job for the wrong age groups.

The bulk of available evidence on the influence of intelligence, early learning, social class, ethnic group, sex, family life, personality and so on is of this depressing nature. The change to interpretative psychology or sociology has switched the focus to factors which teachers can control and which have always been seen as their duty to manage. Once researchers look at the way children give meaning to schooling and learning, to their interactions inside and outside the school, to the way different interpretations of the same situations are reconciled and negotiated, the evidence joins the common-sense knowledge already in use. Interpretative human science produces a different slant on actions already explained by teachers and others because such explanations are a necessary prelude to action. The human scientist's contribution is not necessarily superior, but it is another perspective and, providing the criteria for producing it are followed, may be more dependable as a basis for acting.

The reason why the human sciences are beginning to contribute more to practice can be seen in the limitations imposed on evidence useable by teachers from the experimental designs that were usually used in psychology. Bloom (1976) has pointed out that crucial factors in learning are the previous history of the learners up to the task in hand and their relevant accumulated knowledge. Yet these are the very factors that are often controlled as part of the design of the laboratory experiment on human learning. Children are matched for ability, sex, age, social class, ethnic group so that the effects of the remaining factors are examined. Furthermore, the task given is usually chosen because it is minimally affected by previous learning, even by relying on nonsense words or context-free shapes. Yet the central factor in learning is the previous learning relevant to the task in hand. That is what the learner depends on and the teacher uses. But experimental research controlled this out of account so that the effects of the stimulus being used could be isolated as an influence on learning, uncontaminated by just those factors that are crucial in the classroom. Bloom (1981) has also pointed out that most schooling in the world is still based on the idea that individual ability to learn is fixed and that the task of teachers is steadily to weed out the bad learners. This he compares with the view that, with exceptions at the extreme, there are really faster and slower learners, rather than just good and bad, leading to teaching focused on organising tasks, and the time taken over them, so that all children can master them. This brings teachers the hope and the scope.

The move away from the scientistic model has not been all gain. There are established procedures in experimental and survey research that guide the work and enable readers to check its reliability and validity. That is why scientific papers should include a description of the methods used. If agreement among experts is the ultimate criterion of credibility, then the researcher is under an obligation to publish the methods used. But there are few established methods in interpretative, qualitative research. Even more important, even the most diligently designed and reported observational research has largely to be taken on trust unlike its empiricist predecessor. Sampling procedures, factors measured, statistics calculated can be reported and checked by critics, but it is impossible to know from an account of classroom interaction whether the observations were controlled or merely used to confirm the views of the observer. This is why research such as Bennett's *Teaching Styles and Pupil Progress* (Bennett, 1976) and Rutter's *Fifteen Thousand Hours* (Rutter *et al.*, 1979) received extensive critical reception, but observational studies such as the ORACLE project (Galton and Simon, 1980) escaped the hatchet men.

How do you sort out the Dependable Research Evidence?

It has already been suggested that evidence is given the stamp of approval through publication in high-prestige journals, by the award of a Master's degree or Doctorate, by quotation in works by respected colleagues – in sum, by agreement among those with authority within a discipline. Nevertheless, there are established criteria for judging the quality of research. The reader of a textbook is rarely in a position to follow the sequence of questions involved, but these are useful as guides to informing the scepticism with which texts should be read or lecturers interpreted. These questions reflect criteria, standards that are expected of research. They are not applied rigidly as a check-list, but are in the mind of the assessor as the book, article or thesis is read.

Do the methods used ensure that extraneous factors or bias could not have unduly influenced the results?

This questions reliability. It may be legal to experiment on animals but the limits on constraining humans make it impossible to design human science either to eliminate the influence of researchers, including their political beliefs, or all the many factors that can bias the responses of those being observed or questioned. The reliability of the methods is never perfect.

Do the results really reflect the characteristic or situation under investigation and lead to the conclusions drawn?

This questions validity. Human behaviour and interaction are complicated and researchers often have to use selections, indications, simplifications and substitutes, even when trying to preserve the natural situation. Validity is always questionable. This applies to laboratory experiments as it does to observation of natural events. One can lead to artificiality, the other to selectivity in perception. Furthermore, in both cases the conclusions drawn may not rest on the data collected.

Given the situation in which the research took place and the sample used, can the results be generalised?

This is a difficult question where research is generalised to give advice within education, for observations, experiments, surveys and so on are often concerned with subjects and situations that are not typical of most schools and colleges. It is a familiar criterion to teachers, for models from leafy suburban schools do not necessarily work in the inner cities.

The three questions are closely related. If the methods used are unreliable, yielding different results at different times or with different researchers, the result will not be valid. There is often a choice in research between maximising reliability or validity. First in sociology and then in psychology the trend has been from an emphasis on reliability through controlled experimentation or surveys, to the preservation of the natural situation through using observational, interpretative methods. In sociology the moves towards the preservation of the natural situation go under labels such as ethnography, while in psychology the term ethogenic is used. These qualitative, interpretative approaches share a concern with keeping humans as thinking, active agents at the centre of enquiry, and reporting is often in the words of those being researched. Validity is maximised, but there may be little of the control that adds reliability. In qualitative research unfettered responses are sought. The problem comes in the reporting where the researcher summarises and makes sense of them. Questions on reliability and validity remain important in both traditions.

How can Human Sciences be most profitably applied to Education?

The changing, vulnerable status of theoretical models and the difficulty in obtaining reliable evidence means that caution is necessary in recommending action on the basis of evidence. The temptation is to select the evidence that fits our views of what should be done. The history of education suggests that there is never any difficulty in being convincing in recommending a new approach. Even the twentieth century is littered with breakthroughs that turned out to be dead-ends. Each in their time was backed by evidence claimed to be conclusive. Each was evaluated as a success. For example, whatever happened to the Dalton Plan, first set up in Massachusetts in 1920 by Parkhurst, a student of Montessori, and popular in England later in that decade?[4] Parkhurst gave it the initial boost (Parkhurst, 1922) and Lynch (1924) evaluated it as producing improved results. A more recent example would be the introduction and evaluation of the Initial Teaching Alphabet.[5] Yet that method of teaching reading, which was of major concern in the 1960s, has virtually disappeared from texts and from schools in the eighties.

The ease with which these fashions found support, and the confidence with which they were positively evaluated, suggests that it is difficult to be objective when enthusiastic. The problem arises from the way acceptance of theoretical frameworks colours the way all evidence is interpreted. Perception is structured and it is easy not just to ignore all the counter evidence but to load evaluations to be supportive. This may be unintentional, but it is common. It results in the frequent misuse of words such as proof, confirmation and significance. Such words should always be used and read with caution.

The three questions asked about the status of research tend to lead to dispute rather than agreement. In the end it is the level of agreement among communities of researchers who use and build on the work that decides its acceptability. Because there are competing communities it is usually possible to find evidence that will support very different recommendations for action. Hence we need to add to these three technical criteria when selecting evidence that can be used with confidence to guide teaching. Much of the available evidence has not been produced as a guide to action. Researchers are interested in breakthroughs, in showing that previous work was mistaken or incomplete. They benefit from their iconoclasm because scientific communities reward the imaginative. But those searching for evidence to guide action are looking for the dependable. They support the apparently scientific approach to research because it promises laws and predictions. They are frustrated by the delivery of the tentative and the critical. Thus, while the questions about reliability, validity and generalisability remain important, they have to be extended to produce principles to help teachers and others to pick out the evidence that is a basis for action.

The first principle guiding the selection of theories and evidence in this book is that they should be treated as problematic. They are sources of insight. They can suggest ways of improving or checking professional judgements, but are not substitutes for them. They are simplifications to produce stripped-down models of reality, not reflections of the actual in all its complexity. There is some gap between rats in a maze or monkeys in a cage, or even volunteer psychology students, and children busy in a classroom. The evidence is tentative not conclusive. It is rare for replications to leave conclusions intact. The most famous recent example is the Rosenthal and Jacobson study, *Pygmalion in the Classroom* (1968). Here replications not only failed to obtain raised attainments through raising expectations, but further investigations exposed the frailty of the original study (Elashoff and Snow, 1971).[6]

The second principle used here is to draw on the concepts that have stood the test of time within disciplines. In psychology, individual differences, the active nature of most human learning, the importance of early learning, are such solid foundations. But they also suggest ways of educating more effectively because they can rule out erroneous if common assumptions. Similarly in sociology, the strength of cultural differences, the interaction of economic, political and social factors and the way social interaction is structured are similar solid concepts. Of course, differences of opinion appear as soon as these basic ideas are elaborated or are used as a basis for recommending action within education. But they are powerful ideas and they serve as a base for professional decision-making.

The third principle guiding the writing of this book is that professional judgement should retain an important place in reaching decisions about action. Much of the evidence used to advise teachers is derived from studies that have little to do with classrooms. The researchers will have referred their data to models that are not made explicit when the evidence is borrowed and applied to education. The misunderstandings over the term 'intelligence' and over 'social background' are examples involving over-simplifications in the borrowing. That is the negative reason for coupling judgement to evidence. The positive reason is that one of the most powerful ways of checking the validity and reliability of evidence is triangulation, obtaining it from different sources, by different methods. Teachers can add their own judgement, just as doctors add theirs to the tests they carry out. The second opinion is another way of cross-checking.

The fourth principle is to maximise the use of descriptive evidence that is less likely to be misleadingly interpreted in books and which is suitable for the exercise of judgement within the context of the learning situation. This is low status work in the human sciences, but assessing the use of time and space in the classroom, for example, can be revealing. There are many studies of the way teachers organise learning that rest on no particular human science model, yet are a challenge to the assumption behind the organisation. This theory-free data is still open to distortion and exaggeration. But its status has not been secured in a community closed to teachers and it is open to professional scrutiny.

This chapter has been deliberately critical of the contribution of the human sciences to education. This is not so much the fault of psychologists or sociologists, but of the lax way in which their ideas and evidence have been taken from the theories that give them meaning, and applied as if the evidence was context-free and atheoretical. Looking across the sad history of education affected by notions of innate, unchangeable intelligence, or of rigid stages of development that dictated when learning should be introduced, or of deprivation, social backgrounds, cultures and self-concepts that were used as reasons why children were not learning or could not learn, it is difficult to conclude that the contribution has been beneficial overall. Yet such a balance sheet is nonsense for even if there were no human science, education would be based on notions of motivation, learning and attainment that would be likely to have been more harmful. Indeed the greatest contributions of human scientists have been to undermine harmful and helpless notions such as innate inferiority.

The key to using human science beneficially is to avoid determinism, ideas of rigid causation and to keep on stage the resilience and the individuality of children. There are always exceptions. Individuals and groups break through even the worst conditions. If you see education as part of the state's ideological apparatus designed to mentally subjugate the workers, you can still work to give children the learning that is the key to both subversion and power. Even if you accept that individual consciousness is a reflection of material, class position, you can work to change both. It is unforgiveable to use human science with all its weaknesses as a reason for fatalism. That is why the nature-nurture debate is a waste of time for teachers. If attainment was pre-determined genetically, teaching would be pointless. In practice, humans are capable of breaking any rule, bucking any prediction. That may frustrate social engineers, but it is the hope of optimists.

Thus the obvious question to end this chapter is '*Why does human science play so large a part in educating and advising teachers?*' First, it may be incomplete and sometimes misleading, but it is often the only source of explanation available. Second, in providing an 'external' perspective, human scientists often expose the gap between what people think is happening and what is actually happening. Third, it is often too tempting not to look for the expert. Berger (1961) put it this way: 'There remains something in all of us of the childish belief that there is a world of grown-ups who know. There must be because we, evidently, don't know.' We can learn a great deal from human sciences. However, much will never be found out about an issue as complicated as the organisation of learning in the classroom that is the subject of this book. Yet as teachers we have to act. The remaining chapters look at the research basis for that action in relation to classroom learning.

NOTES

1   A similar example of a community with shared criteria for evaluation is Her Majesty's Inspectors (HMI). They are organised into a hierarchy, carefully select and induct new members, and have developed their own criteria for producing and publishing evidence. These criteria for evaluating schooling change as rapidly as those used in academia. Thus the evaluation of primary schooling in the Plowden Report of 1967 (DES, 1967) differs markedly from that in the survey a decade later, *Primary Education in England and Wales* (DES, 1978), in the criteria used to judge effectiveness.

2   Social scientists are roughly divisible into those adopting a 'top-down' and those adopting a 'bottom-up' approach. The former are often labelled positivist, empiricist, scientist or behaviourist. They are modelled on the natural sciences, imposing theories, concepts, definitions, categories, labels on human behaviour in advance of investigation. The methods used are comparison, survey, questioning, testing and experimenting. The results are usually quantitative. 'Bottom-up' approaches are interpretative, focused on the meanings that humans give to social situations. The methods used are usually observational and the results qualitative. There is great variety among these interpretive approaches and the groups tend to work under exotic titles. In sociology these include social interactionism, symbolic interactionism and social phenomenology.

3   Social scientists make their models explicit. The reader can usually see why explanations follow from the evidence presented because the model is the source of the interpretation of data. But everyone

uses models, albeit implicitly. In these cases the reader or listener has no way of seeing why conclusions are being drawn.

4   The Dalton Plan was introduced into Dalton High School, Massachusetts in 1920 and soon spread across the US and into the UK. It consists of individual work guided by worksheets and assignment cards. The children worked independently or in groups, taking responsibility for their own learning.

5   The Initial Teaching Alphabet (ita) consists of 44 instead of 26 symbols. It was designed by Sir James Pitman to overcome the problems in learning to read by ensuring close relations between visual symbol and spoken word. It was widely used in the 1960s and 1970s.

6   The *Pygmalion in the Classroom* study (Rosenthal and Jacobson, 1968) presented evidence suggesting that teachers could raise the attainment of children by having high expectations of them. It became very popular in promising that raising self-image, teaching with a smile and avoiding labelling was not only effective but easy to introduce. The evidence was quickly incorporated into teacher education. Unfortunately most researchers replicating the study were unable to obtain the expected gains in learning and an investigation of the experiment revealed a degree of unreliability that suggested that the evidence was useless (Elashoff and Snow, 1971). While it is obviously more promising to expect high attainment as a teacher, keep smiling and to try to boost rather than depress children, it is necessary to be aware that planning and effectiveness take a lot of work, particularly when the social background of the children is taken into account.

2 From Learning Theories to Models for Teaching

In Chapter 1 the focus was on the relation between theoretical models, research design and the evidence produced. Now the concern will be with one cluster of models developed to try to understand human learning. These will be examined for the messages they contain about the best way of organising learning in the classroom. This is an absurdly ambitious task. Yet learning theories should guide practice and traditionally they have been a prominent part of courses in teacher education. Justifiably this approach has been described as 'galloping through the gurus' (Stones, 1984). Yet the different models have informed teaching and the experimental evidence is important.

The fundamental point is that psychologists, sociologists and teachers are all concerned with how people learn and all use models as sources of hunches and hypotheses. Hence there is overlap across the different approaches, even if this has to be sought out. Teachers may only model implicitly but even the most elementary planning of a lesson will involve some picture in the mind of the task in hand, the abilities of the children and the appropriate strategies for successful organisation. Psychologists may model human behaviour or thinking more systematically in order to derive hypotheses for testing, and sociologists may model human interaction in order to select aspects for observation, but each is engaged in the same process, taking into account similar factors.

The approach used in this chapter has been heavily influenced by Joyce and Weil (1980) who organise learning theories into families that can inform repertoires for teachers to learn and use. Behind this is an important assumption that apparently conflicting theories are in reality complementary, dealing with different aspects of learning rather than reaching opposed conclusions about learning as a whole. This assumption rests on an easily misunderstood aspect of attempts to model learning. None tells us how learning actually occurs in the mind. Cognitive psychologists model the processes. Behaviourists ignore them and concentrate on the outcomes rather than the thinking. But none can spell out how learning occurs. It is still useful to know that some stimuli are more effective than others, or that feedback can aid problem-solving. You don't have to know how the human mind works to manage learning most effectively. But remembering that limitation is a useful reminder that dogmatism is out of place in this essentially speculative area.

There has been heavy investment by psychologists and sociologists in the investigation of three aspects of human learning. These contrasting approaches often seem to yield conflicting evidence to teachers interested in increasing the effectiveness of the organisation of learning. The differences are explicable in terms of the assumptions about the human mind used in the research, the focus of that work and the methods employed in collecting the evidence. The message of Chapter 1 has to be remembered. What comes out of research is the product of what is put into the design.

The table below summarises the differences in the three approaches. These have fuelled a century of dispute within the human sciences. But it has to be remembered that each approach is to the same complicated process of learning. Here they are treated as complementary in order to extract the evidence that seems reliable and valid so that it can be used to guide practice.

Three approaches to learning

Approach	Model used: humans as	Focus for research on	View of learning as
Behaviourist	Machines	Products	Incremental
Cognitive	Systems	Processes	Insightful
Personal/ Social	Searchers for meanings	Social relations	Interactive

These approaches are elaborated in all standard books on learning or educational psychology. For example, Bigge (1982) lists ten theories of learning, each with its accompanying psychological viewpoint, conception of humanity, basis for the transfer of learning, emphasis in teaching and key supporters today and in history. Joyce and Weil (1980) list 22 learning models to produce a basic repertoire of approaches for teachers.

Here the intention is not to summarise more than one hundred years of research, but to extract the evidence that has come to be assumed as dependable in order to relate it to the way teachers organise learning in the classroom, this being the subject of Chapters 3, 4 and 5.

Behaviourist Models

Psychology developed as an experimental science at the end of the nineteenth century by concentrating on the observable behaviour produced by stimulating animals and human subjects under controlled laboratory conditions. This remains a powerful tradition and the evidence produced has the merit of all experimental science, confidence that causes have been identified for particular effects because extraneous influences have been controlled. The basic model is as follows.

$$\text{Stimulus or input} \longrightarrow \text{Response or output}$$

Note first that the concern is with the impact of the stimulus on behaviour (response), not with what goes on in the mind when stimulated. These are sometimes named Connectionist or Stimulus-Response theories. Second, the research was often carried out on dogs, rats, pigeons and so on, rather than on humans who are less amenable when subjected to electric shocks or starved to increase the stimulation of the sight of food. Pavlov's dogs were taught to salivate at the sound of a bell, and Skinner taught pigeons to walk in a figure of eight and rats to press levers to obtain food.[1] Thus the conclusions from this work apply to simple skill learning.

Two key conclusions have emerged from this work and been taken into the repertoire of all teachers. First, the strength of the bond between stimulus and response is increased by practice. If a newly learned skill is not practised it is likely to be lost. It did not need psychologists to tell this to teachers who are regularly getting children to practise their multiplication tables or spellings or shoelace knotting. Second, learning depends on the reward of successful performances. Once again, teachers are skilled in handing out praise for success, criticism for failure. Psychologists have elaborated procedures that are in common use. This was to be expected. They were looking at the same phenomena as teachers. What Pavlov, Thorndike, Skinner and others did was to give precision to practices already in use, to show the limits within which they could be effective and to show the inefficiency of many current procedures. A good example has been Skinner's criticisms of classroom practices and the lack of reinforcement experienced by most children (Skinner, 1968).

The importance of this behaviourist research can be illustrated by looking at the evidence on memory. Most of what we read or hear goes into a short-term memory and is rapidly forgotten. A little may pass into the long-term memory. There is a rapid falling away of the curve of memory (Ebbinhaus, 1966). The experimental evidence yields ways of reducing the loss. This can be done by:

a   ensuring that the span of attention required of children is short enough to hold their attention so that they don't have too many lapses in which new and previous information will be lost;

b   inserting questions, repetitions, visual aids to reinforce the learning and reduce the gap between short- and long-term memory;

c   linking new knowledge to that already of interest to children so they can relate to and hence practise it;

d   using new information in practical work, or as a basis for illustration or discussion, or acting;

e   by over-learning the skill through repetition;

f   by avoiding interference with the learning required (This can come either through prior or later learning which gets in the way. In both cases interference is likely when the two learning tasks are similar and close in time.);

g   by organising revision at regular intervals. This will not only reduce the chance of forgetting, but provide the opportunity for re-learning information already lost.

Behaviourist theories also remain influential in particular approaches to learning. Programmed learning, for example, rests on the continuous use of reinforcement to motivate further learning. Most structured learning packages are behaviourist in origin. Thus the DISTAR programme is carefully structured so that new stimuli are presented only when a desired response has been given to a previous stimulus (Englemann, Osborn and Englemann, 1972).[3] The teacher controls the rewards that reinforce, although these may be negotiated with children to increase their attraction. Training programmes used in industry and the military services are similar in organisation. Exercises are carefully sequenced and success is reinforced immediately. Behaviour modification is another similar technique depending on the provision of rewards and sometimes punishments to promote approved responses especially where there have been discipline problems. However, structured programmes using selected stimuli, sequenced, short-step learning and planned reinforcement are only the tip of the management of learning iceberg: they try to control behaviour rather than understand how people learn or actively promote their own learning.

Cognitive or Information Processing Models

An obvious criticism of experiments that face rats with limited choices in a maze or box under the close scrutiny of psychologists is that little beyond trial and error learning should be expected, as the situation is somewhat alien to the beast. While many psychologists pursued experimental rigour in the laboratory, others were observing animals and humans in their natural habitat. Often what they saw was not incremental learning whereby simple skills were mastered and used to build more complex ones, but insights without apparent aggregation. This school of psychology is usually referred to as *Gestalt*, meaning whole or configuration.

It is significant that the *Gestalt* psychologists tended to be German in origin. They saw contemplative learning where their American peers saw rats, dogs and pigeons with a get-up-and-go, trial and error approach. The perception seems to have depended on cultural background. Not surprisingly therefore the developments in electronic systems, range-finding, radar and computing have produced a recent growth area in cognitive science and information technology where the focus is on information processing with systems that are adaptive and with the human mind as capable of using information, particularly feedback from actions instigated.

In these information-processing models there is an active human, not a responder to external stimuli that condition behaviour. The action is often exploratory, corner-cutting, apparently irrational in search of solutions. This isn't a machine but an ingenious inventor. At its simplest the model used is an elementary system such as this feedback loop.

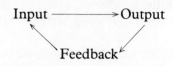

However, caution is necessary in accepting such a simplified model, just as it is in simple stimulus-response images. The models are from information systems and to speak of knowledge structures, drives, cognitive maps and feedback is to suggest something concrete. In practice, the models serve as sources of hypotheses not as descriptions of the human mind. Behaviourists and cognitive psychologists share this dependence on models. But neither should be taken as a picture of the way the mind works.

The key conclusions for teachers in this concentration on cognition are that opportunities must be given for insights to occur and that these require organisation. The teaching job is to provide the tasks and the tools to promote understanding. That comes through individual activity, but the prior enquiry, experiment, evaluation and generalisation need to be organised. These need to be set at a level appropriate for the stage of development reached. The teacher needs to be aware of the nature of the task, the attainments brought to it by the children, its appropriateness to their experience and maturity, and the ways in which what is known to the children can be used to encourage them to probe the unknown.

This focus on cognition frees the researcher from the restraints of the laboratory. The major developmental psychologist of this century, Jean Piaget, relied on observation in natural surroundings. Much modern work involves observation of humans interfacing with machines, particularly computers. The gain has not just been to stop relying on the behaviour of animals in artificial surroundings as a source of insight into human learning, but to extend investigation into high-level, complex learning. The loss has been in the control exercised in these investigations. Much of Piaget's work has been shown to have been influenced by the limited range of children he observed, his own training as a biologist and the nature of the tasks set for the children (Cohen, 1983; Brown and Desforges, 1979).

Social Interaction Models

Teachers are concerned with more than the learning of new knowledge and skills. Indeed, that learning often depends on children feeling secure as persons within an environment that is supportive. The concern with the quality of social interaction is once again shared by teachers and human scientists. Here psychologists, social psychologists and sociologists have developed models of the way humans interact, and through that interaction learn about themselves. This, and the language through which most interaction occurs, is the subject of Chapter 3.

The most influential models concentrated on the person have been developed by therapists such as Rogers (1951).[3] The Nondirective Counselling Model lies behind many pastoral care arrangements and is designed to help pupils explore their own lives in relation to others. They are assumed to be responsible for their own learning. This assumption is poles apart from the behaviourist model of the relation of stimulus to response. Thus in a model modestly entitled *Joy: Expanding Human Awareness* (Schutz, 1967), there is more prescription than description, more hope than evidence, despite the scientific language used.

Similar utopian exercises can be found in models of social interaction. First, there are those devised from a conception of the good society. They range from Plato's *Republic*, through the work of visionaries such as Marcuse,[4] to plain nutters. Most conclude that the good society, being democratic, rests on democracy in schools. The temptation is to relate classroom practices such as group activity, collaboration and child-centredness to the influence of the Great and Good. But, once again, it is wise to be cautious. Teachers are concerned with the same range of issues as social and political thinkers and there is no necessary connection between Dewey's *Democracy and Education* (1916) and the co-operative organisation of British primary schools in the 1980s.[5]

There is however one very important model of human relations and the development of consciousness that lies behind much of the evidence in contemporary literature on education. It spans psychology and sociology. At its heart is the view of human beings as actively seeking to understand the world around them. The comparison of this model of the human with that in the behaviourist tradition holds the clue to the way the evidence on education has changed. From a concern with observable behaviour and a neglect of the meanings given to the situation observed by the subject, the focus has been switched to the way humans interpret their world and hence respond to it. Even more important, these interpretations apply in particular to other people who are the most important parts of the action. The teacher is now advised to attend to the impact of her actions on the self-concept of the pupils. They are modelled as interacting, negotiating, active interpreters of learning, not as passive recipients. This is a dramatic switch in the way teaching and learning in the classroom are conceived. But the switch also informs the design of the research as described in Chapter 1. Once again it is unbalanced to argue that evidence produces changes in practice. Human scientists and teachers now employ models of learning that emphasise activity and interpretation. But there is no necessary precedence to the former as pioneer. Both have been involved in improving material conditions in classrooms that make more activity possible.

The Practical Implications of Evidence on Learning

Taking the four guides to using evidence presented at the end of Chapter 1 (pages 14–16), six broad areas of agreement can be identified with sufficient consistency and permanence to make them a credible basis for use. These six points refer to different stages of learning. Points 1 and 2 are concerned with learners bringing to the task very different accumulations of knowledge, and attitudes and skills that can make the learning hard or easy, rewarding or frustrating, necessitating attention by the teacher to both organisation and motivation. Points 3 and 4 refer to the way learning involves active engagement and can be promoted and consolidated. Points 5 and 6 warn that because learning is active, involving both social interaction and exciting if unpredictable conclusions among children in classrooms, it should not be constrained to the point of inhibiting either collaboration or spontaneity. These last two points are elaborated in Chapters 5 and 7.

1 Whether child- or teacher-centred, learning in classrooms is organised

Learning theories model the way the individual is observed to behave when engaged on a task. In the end the learning takes place in the mind and the processes at work can only be guessed at. Hence the focus is on the relation between factors in the classroom, the home and so on and others assumed to be at work inside the mind of the learner and on the stimuli presented. The practical implications of all such theories can be spelled out as optimum conditions for learning. Learning can be random, but if specified steps are followed, it can be made more effective. The nature of the task and the characteristics of the learners are both important factors in deciding on the most effective way of organising learning. But the models all point to possibilities of such optimal organisation.

It is possible to overlook the importance of the organisation of learning, especially if the methods recommended are informal. The Plowden Report's conclusion that '. . . the child is the agent in his own learning' was followed by a repetition of the comment from the Hadow Report of 1931 that '. . . the curriculum is to be thought of in terms of activity and experience rather than of knowledge to be acquired and facts to be stored' (DES, 1967, paragraph 529). Activity and experience are stressed as the keys to learning. Instruction is seen to bewilder children in many primary schools because it can outrun their experience. But making learning suitable for the experience of the children still requires organisation. While the assumption in the Report is that children have a natural urge to explore and discover, this is seen as fulfilled through '. . . a carefully prepared environment in which choices and interest are supported by their teachers, who will have in mind the potentialities for further learning' (paragraph 530).

The features implicit in the Plowden approach to the organisation of learning are that the environment for the activity of children has to be carefully prepared to encourage motivation. The work should be matched to the development of the children. It should be paced so that they are not lost or bored. The new should be based on the familiar. While a rigid division into subjects can hinder learning, the job of the teacher is to help children to see the order and pattern in experience. The agenda below the support for activity among children is of learning as organised, sequenced, paced and firmly teacher-controlled. The evidence of the developments in the primary schools since the publication of the Plowden Report in 1967 is that most teachers never made any other assumptions about their responsibility. They remained firmly in control of the learning activities in the classroom, regardless of the formality or informality of the action (Boydell, 1981; Simon, 1981; King, 1978; Bennett *et al.*, 1984).

2   Cues, clues and advanced organisers as essential motivation

The second aspect of the organisation of learning that recurs in various models is an emphasis on motivation as an essential introduction to the task. Once again all teachers use some form of this advanced organisation. They frequently tell the children what is to be learned or done and then spell out how this is to be done. This assumption that effective learning is promoted by making it clear what is going to go on may be neglected or undervalued, just as it is possible to forget that the spontaneous activity of children may not lead to any worthwhile learning unless it is guided. Hence many learning theories have a practical value in stressing the promotion of motivation as an important factor.

At its simplest the cue may be a reminder of what was covered last time, a quick revision or a brief outline of what is going to happen next. The presentation and preparation of the work to come can be elaborated to enthuse the children, get them set. But there is also the Advanced Organiser Model which employs the main concepts to be covered in an abstract form as an introduction to the learning itself (Ausubel, 1963). This is more than just a preview. It is designed to identify in advance the key aspects and attributes of the work to follow. Examples will be given, with the context in which they are to be found. The ideas and the examples are explored by the teachers and children. This is a unit of work designed to organise the knowledge available to learners so that the new material to follow will be meaningful. Thus there is a range of cues used from simple to complex. The common feature is that learning is enhanced when there is preparation through stimulating the recall of relevant knowledge and fixing it in the mind in advance of the new being presented.

3   Reinforcement as the cement of learning

Theories all tend to stress or assume that the rewarding of success and the discouragement of failure are central to effective learning. There is a long history of research showing how the frequency and recency of rewards make a difference. These have been most marked among behaviourists, and the way reinforcement is built into learning can be seen most clearly in programmed learning. Here the rewards are not only given quickly after successful responses, but the learning is itself broken down into short steps to maximise the use of such rewards. Once again this reinforcement can be seen in the actions of teachers as they go about encouraging children in the classroom. The quick word of encouragement, a caution that it is not good enough, a tick or a cross on the work are the stock-in-trade of teaching. There may be a problem because the rewards may be used selectively and some children may miss them. The work may be organised so that the gap between completion of a task and its evaluation may be too wide, but teachers have an implicit realisation of the importance of quickly feeding-back evidence of success or failure.

The importance of reinforcement can also be seen in the attempt to shorten the time between performance and assessment in the school careers of children. Continuous assessment, graded tests, mastery learning, records, check-lists and profiles are all attempts to move from summary, summative assessment after work has been finished and little can be done about it, to formative assessment wherein information can be fed back to the learner and to teachers as the work is progressing. This is partly to guide both learner and teacher, but also to motivate the former and to give information on past performance as a guide to the future.[6]

4   Practice, participation and application

Learning, remembering and using what has been learned depend on activity that not only consolidates but rehearses and gives meaning. This can be seen not only in rote learning, but in the more complicated higher level activities where new material is related by the learner to the knowledge and ideas already possessed. Knowledge and skills may be learned by a concentration on simplified exercises, but it is their practice and application that establishes them as part of a repertoire that can be used in a variety of situations.

Once again, this organised practice and application can be seen in the way teachers arrange classroom activities, or in the layout of textbooks. Skills are taught before the pupils are encouraged to tackle open-ended tasks which involve them. Activity is encouraged. To the Plowden Committee this priority arose from a natural urge in children to explore. But it is also part of every teacher's armoury as a means of extending knowledge, skills and attitudes. Activity is essential in learning because it can lead to the new being understood through being related to existing knowledge.

All learning theories contain this emphasis on practice. There is a spectrum from repetitive rote learning to helping children to build concepts into schema which can be used to tackle new and complicated tasks. This range from basic to sophisticated, from memorising to problem-solving can be appreciated in this advice to mathematics teachers.

> . . . try to lay a well-structured foundation of basic mathematical ideas, on which the learner can build in whatever future direction becomes necessary: that is, to find for oneself, and help one's pupils to find, the basic patterns. Secondly, to teach them always to be looking for these for themselves: and thirdly, to teach them always to accommodate their schemas – to appreciate the values of these as working tools, but always to be willing to replace them by better ones. The first of these is teaching mathematics, the second and third are teaching pupils to learn mathematics. Only these last prepare pupils for an unknown future.
>
> Skemp (1971, page 53)

5 Learning as negotiation as well as transmission

A look at children's exercise books or overhearing them discussing a lesson soon banishes the image in most writing on learning of the passive, accurate reception of knowledge. There will not only be misunderstandings but interpretations. Many of these will be based in profound beliefs, established outside the school and varying with the social backgrounds of the children. Even the youngest child will interpret the teaching given. This aspect of learning is the concern of sociologists as well as psychologists. It is the subject of Chapter 3.

The active interpretation of classroom activity by children relating it to values, to knowledge, to perceptions established in family and community raises moral issues. Teachers have to decide how far they have a responsibility to promote a common culture and how far to encourage diversity. That is an issue for philosophers (for example, Dearden, 1968) and for curriculum theorists (for example, Lawton, 1975). It is also of immediate concern in the organisation of learning. In some areas of work such as mathematics, there may be few conflicts of meanings over the concepts and skills introduced. But there may still be different perceptions of the importance of content, for example, between boys and girls. In other areas such as history or geography or language, children may give very different meanings to the same events when compared to those of the teacher or their classmates. It is easy to exaggerate this relative aspect of knowledge. The accumulated discoveries of humanity have to be transmitted to each new generation. Yet these are integrated by individuals into their own cognitive structures. That always involves interpretation of the message and often negotiation with the teacher.

6   Not all learning can or should be organised

A repetitive theme of this chapter has been that human learning is complicated while models of it are necessarily simplified. Teachers can use these models to improve the possibilities of successful learning by producing the right environment. But the learning is achieved by the child and there may be many individual approaches to it. This is a reason for allowing children scope to develop their own approach to, extension and application of work presented. We know too little not to depend on individuals playing an active and spontaneous part within any organisation of learning.

There is however an even more important and positive reason for allowing young children scope for individuality. It is not just that we do not know how they learn, it is that they often go about it in their own serious, sustained and imaginative ways. A look at Armstrong's *Closely Observed Children* (Armstrong, 1980) will confirm this point. Watching young children writing, drawing, playing and so on he records the 'high intent' in their activity. They were absorbed emotionally as well as intellectually as they worked and played. Justifiably he talks of them 'appropriating' knowledge. This is a long way from pacing, sequencing and structuring by the teacher. The learning environment still has to be organised, but within it, whether defined as work or play, children are finding their own solutions, exercising their own imaginations, in a serious endeavour to acquire knowledge. Such motivation might not last, but it is precious while it does. It should be encouraged, not squeezed out by a rigid curriculum.

NOTES

1   I. Pavlov (1849–1936) was a Russian famous for experiments producing conditioned reflexes in dogs. The work was a major influence on the development of behaviourism in psychology.

B. F. Skinner (born 1904) was a major figure in behavioural psychology in America and a critic of methods in education, particularly the failure to reinforce learning in the classroom (see Note 6 below).

2   DISTAR is a high structure language programme developed in the US and aimed at teaching children who find methods requiring high motivation or ability very difficult. It is used in special education or with children with special educational needs. Direct teaching seems to produce at least short-term gains, but ignoring developmental status runs counter to most teachers' views of the best way of helping children to read, speak and write.

3   Carl Rogers was born in 1903 and developed ideas on non-directive therapy and teaching. This is the opposite of behaviourism and of programmes such as DISTAR above. The counsellor or teacher does not direct the child but facilitates self-directed initiatives, thus encouraging responsibility for self-learning (Rogers, 1951).

4   Herbert Marcuse worked at the Frankfurt Institute of Social Research before moving to the US following the rise of the Nazis in Germany. Writing from the University of California he became a guru for the hippy generation in the 1960s and the eco-nuts of the 1970s through his support for a revolution in humanity's relations to nature as part of the necessary attack on capitalism in the Western world.

5   The tendency in books to relate current developments in schooling to the influence of the Great and Good in the distant past is unfortunate. Dewey was an American philosopher concerned with the role that schools could play in supporting democracy. Exporting such ideas to contemporary England might be misleading. J. J. Rousseau lived in the middle of the eighteenth century and

has been connected with the rise of naturalism, naturism, democracy, fascism, dictatorship as well as progressive primary education. The reason for his ubiquity lies in the brilliance and breadth of his writing. It is worth remembering that his view that children are naturally good, as expressed in books such as *Emile*, is developed in a pre-industrial pastoral paradise, far removed from contemporary urban, industrial conditions and from Rousseau's callous treatment of his own children.

6 See Note 1 above. Skinner's views on reinforcement as the key to learning have been heavily criticised. But teachers do not find it easy to provide the quick evidence of success or failure that can encourage correct and inhibit incorrect learning.

3 Social and Linguistic Factors in Learning[1]

So far, the way knowledge is organised into a curriculum, is taught and evaluated has been treated as evidently a good thing for all concerned. But learning is communication and the knowledge acquired brings power. The curriculum and the organisation of learning could be organised very differently under extreme Left or Right wing regimes. In any classroom, teacher and pupils are unlikely to share identical values and views. In this chapter learning is considered as active, interactive, negotiated, rather than the passive and individual reception of unproblematic messages.[2]

This view of learning as human interaction is radical in challenging not only the apparent purposes of communication in education but the very nature of the curriculum that is being communicated. It applies to the relations between teachers and children and to the way these are organised. Thus Edwards and Furlong (1978) have shown how teaching and learning, like all social interaction, require children to suspend their own meanings and to adopt those of the teacher. In the classroom it is assumed that children will not know something until they have grasped it in the way the teacher has defined it. Especially with young children, the assumption is that they have to switch into the set of meanings given, the explanations offered. Similarly King (1978), looking at infant classrooms, has shown how teachers defined what was to count as play, what was a 'proper' painting, what was real. Teachers chose reading books, told stories, set writing tasks and number work, and in doing so were emphasising their definition of what was real, important and worthwhile.

The radicalism of this view of knowledge as defined, constructed and valued as part of education applies to the very categories that are used to organise learning and to evaluate children. Teachers typify and classify children to explain their attainment or motivation and to adjust work set to individual characteristics. That is 'good practice'. But the concepts used, such as 'intelligence', 'readiness', 'attainment', 'deprived', 'self-image' and so on are also, in this view, socially constructed. Squibb (1973) has shown how this was done in the case of the term 'intelligence' up to the late 1960s. Children were categorised, selected, streamed using tests and judgements based on a definition of intelligence as innate and unchanging throughout life. Twenty years later this seems obscene. Yet the definition now rejected went unchallenged for generations, supported by the social construction of the concept and the way this blinkered those who elaborated and used it.

These are controversial and complex subjects within sociology and socio-linguistics. All the cautions about the influences on the research and the interpretations of the evidence produced have to be remembered. It is easy to state that communication is learning as well as a vehicle for learning, or that language and thinking are inseparable, or that reality is defined through social interaction, or that different social classes use different linguistic codes. But statements such as these raise many problems and solve few. A useful summary of the difficulties in interpreting the evidence can be found in Stubbs (1983). It is an important topic because teaching is about talking. The ideas can be exciting, intoxicating. But the whole area lacks the concrete base of repeated research that can eventually produce evidence that is sound enough for sober evaluation and application. That is not to challenge its usefulness. That lies in the search for understanding social life. It is a warning against confusing this speculation and model-building with evidence that is a firm basis for prediction and application.

So far, the view taken of children as learners in the classroom has been psychological. Even where these have taken the learning child as active, that activity has been explained by factors in the present, by the way the context for learning has been organised, its introduction, stimulation and reinforcement. There have been few references to the past history of the children and the different views they bring to the learning situation. Indeed, it has already been argued that the way psychologists control their experiments on learning often eliminates consideration of factors such as social class, culture, or perceptions of the way the world is organised from consideration as possible influences on learning. Because the focus is on individual psychological factors, those of sociological interest are often eliminated as possible causes.

In theory as well as practice, perception, and hence learning, is not only influenced by past experience, but by the way knowledge is defined, valued and exchanged. We are now a long way from rats in a cage and from humans as individual information processors. We are looking for the way they come to interpret the world around them, particularly the actions of other humans. The focus is on the meanings given by different groups to similar events, for it is possible not only to detect individual differences in interpretation, but to identify distinctive views among specific groups.

The common sociological variables of social class, gender, ethnic group, occupation and age are significant because they point to the defining characteristics of groups that often have very different views of the political, social and economic implications of events.[3] Children will bring to the classroom views of the worth of school knowledge that may vary according to their experience in the home and local community. These views are likely to contrast with those of teachers. If they have to be suspended in order to learn academic meanings, the personal cost can be high. In trying to show how this occurs, it is too easy to ignore the differences within groups of children and teachers. Furthermore, a different set of factors from those identifying other groups would be likely to produce different views of the world. Rich and poor, girls and boys, Muslims and Jews, lawyers and their clients, young and old, will draw on different stocks of knowledge and belief to interpret their interaction. We rarely know everything about other people. Further, we often unintentionally conceal the bases of our claim to be experts. Doctors, politicians and priests, like teachers, benefit from the mystery of their craft, for this boosts their credentials.

In society as a whole there is clearly a stock of human knowledge that is developed, maintained and transmitted to a degree that enables us to live together despite our differences. In the classroom where knowledge is at the heart of the business, there is communication signifying common elements in the perceptions of teacher and learners, but also misunderstanding and conflict. The effort to transmit knowledge makes this consideration of the way it is built into each human mind particularly important. If the content of the lesson appears common sense, useful and ethical to the teacher while seeming nonsense, useless and insulting to the children, there is a more important point than the organisation of learning. This more profound issue has to be faced. There may be more than one definition of worthwhile knowledge and reconciliation or negotiation may have to precede transmission if it is to be effective. Learning becomes part of social interaction. The provision of stimuli is of less importance than factors such as power to determine who can impose his or her definitions on whom.

Ths Social Construction of Reality

If reality consists of individual perceptions, how can social relations have the predictability that enables us to co-exist, communicate and learn (see Berger and Luckmann, 1961)? A start to unravelling how people give their world meaning is to accept that most of us have some consistency in that interpretation. We act predictably in most circumstances because of that consistent view of the way things are ordered. Clearly much of that stability comes from the way the world around us appears as objective reality. We experience it as given. We learn to respond to it from our interactions with other people and with material objects. Much of this objective world, apparently external to us, is experienced as sets of expectations. We learn to respond and hence interact smoothly. Indeed, the predictability of much of our social behaviour is remarkable. Even young children have an extensive repertoire of social skills that others can depend on. It is when a child fails to shake when offered a hand or barges his way to the front of the queue for milk that the dependence of social relations on the learning that produces predictability in behaviour becomes clear.

The sociological interest in the way humans give meaning to the situations they face has produced a counter-balance to the view of learning as a passive product of expectations by adults for children. It brings into focus areas where those involved interpret and then reconcile their views with those of others. The different social constructions of reality are negotiated, or one or other is imposed. But the attempt at imposition is still likely to leave the contrary interpretation intact, particularly if it is embedded in values in family or community. Many problems in school learning spring from this clash. The strength of social

background factors in the determination of attainment is par-
tially the result of the strength given to children to resist
definitions of situations that violate those held by family and
friend.

There is clearly a difference in the capacity of children to
counter the teacher's definition of reality as they get older. For
the baby the world is objective reality. In the infant class the
teacher is in a position to correct, reject and instruct without
meeting established counter-definitions. Yet even here all things
are not always bright and beautiful. King (1978) in a study of
three infant classrooms not only documents resistance by the
children to the standards of the teachers, but examines the
explanation used for the problems. Teachers pointed to the
social background of the children in the social priority school
studied, and the school log-book showed that this explanation
had been in use for at least forty years. Yet these young children
could still be told that this was how the world was. With older
children there is likely to be a firmer base from which alternative
interpretations can be derived to oppose those given by teachers.

This idea of reality as created by humans is very old. Its
sociological roots go back to W. I. Thomas (1928) who coined
the phrase 'definition of the situation'. On this view what is real
is that which is defined as real. Thus, teaching can be seen as the
definition of reality for children. This has been shown to apply
even when the philosophy expressed by teachers is child-centred
(Sharp and Green, 1975). The instructions, questions and
classroom organisation were ways of keeping order and of
imposing an adult definition of reality on the children.
Furthermore, below the principles and practices in the classroom lay the powers vested in teachers. The negotiation is
inevitably present in the classroom, given the different
backgrounds among children and between them and the teacher.
But adult life is made tolerable inside and outside the classroom
only if children are taught some measure of approved behaviour.

The emphasis in this chapter has been on the face-to-face
interaction that is part of all human learning. At the centre of this
approach that spans sociology and social psychology lies the
model of a reflexive individual capable of thinking out actions
after giving meaning to situations faced. On this view we act,
learning according to the way we interpret the world around us.
That is a long way from the sociology described in Chapter 1
which was based on surveys, comparisons and experiments.

Once again it is necessary to return to the models behind the evidence. A survey-based study such as Bennett (1976) is liable to arrive at very different conclusions from another study such as the ORACLE project (Galton and Simon, 1980),[4] or Bennett's later work, largely based on observation (Bennett et al., 1980, 1984) Similarly, there are two traditions in sociology, one looking at individual interpretations of events, the other at concepts and categories such as socialisation, social control, social class and social mobility. These categories impose meanings on the situation surveyed through the questions asked and the coding of the responses.

Despair may be a reasonable response to such discrepancies within the same subject, but is not necessary. First, sociologists, like other human scientists, tend to use a variety of methods, both observational and survey-based, when approaching a particular issue. So do educational researchers such as Bennett or Galton. The problem often invites a variety of approaches. Second, it would be absurd if the two approaches led to one version of humanity as active interpretors, while the other led to the same people seeming to be passive responders. The reason why these conflicting perspectives rarely appear is that the meaning given to many events by one person is likely to be similar to that given by others. To survive we have to interpret everyday events in ways that enable us to interact with others. Deviance may appear to be rife and is rightly a subject for social scientific study. But even the deviant has to carry out routine interactions with other people. Young children may often be naughty, but their survival depends on learning to respond to clues and cues given by parents and teachers, and to give the appropriate messages to adults in return!

In a similar way, an interpretation of education as socialisation, as a means for allocating life chances or as part of the ideological state apparatus still leaves children acting in individual and often annoying ways in classrooms. If schools are organised to exert social control or ensure the quiescence of the working class, or an obedient, skilled labour force, many teachers and pupils must be acting subversively to break the system. In reality they, and all of us, interpret events individually. But that interpretation takes account of our dependence on others. One sociological approach is the complement of the other, for humans are like hedgehogs, needing to be close, but spikey in their intimacy.

Language in the Classroom

Many observers in classrooms have interpreted the verbal interaction between teachers and children as a form of colonization or subordination. Teachers consistently correct, re-phase, reject and extend contributions from children to teach the approved codes. Barnes, for example, has shown how teachers organise communication in the classroom to control and change the meanings that children bring to school (Barnes, 1979). Often the teacher's language acts as a barrier to learning because it is abstract. Children may understand the problem under discussion, but fail to contribute because their expression of it is rejected by, or misunderstood by, the teacher. To Barnes, the use of abstract language to explain complicated ideas is often confused with its use to support the status of teachers as experts. Through the use of a special language, teachers impose their definitions of situations and simultaneously establish their authority.

Here is another powerful explanation of the passive learning observed in the classroom studies reported in Chapter 5 (pages 76-8). The typical primary classroom may be organised in groups and the work may be individualised, but the children are learning established definitions of the world around them. That is essential in many areas of the curriculum. But in many others there is no one way, no single interpretation. Indeed, children are often asked to think out the problem for themselves. But the worksheet, the marking and above all the interaction over the questions and their answers, diminishes the children's interpretations of the reasons for celebrating Christmas or for Henry VIII having six wives. The consequence is to bring children to accept their world rather than to make it, to receive knowledge passively rather than coming to master and extend it.

Barnes argues that children should be encouraged to construct their own reality, to interpret for themselves. This could be achieved by organising small group discussion, by promoting self-responsible learning. There is some evidence that even seven and eight year olds are capable of discussing topics responsibly so that self-learning occurs (Rosen and Rosen, 1973). Group discussion was strongly recommended by the Plowden Committee. Yet the evidence from the ORACLE project suggests that collaborative group work is rare, and that

although groups are the dominant form of classroom organisation, the work is done individually.

Barnes also recommends listening to children in the classroom. Given the logistic difficulties, this would require listening
in a whole class or group situation. Listening to individuals is
liable to be too brief to be of much use. But in a class or group
situation, the teacher is liable to control the communication both
to determine the meanings transmitted and to maintain authority, however strong the commitment to child-centredness. This
is probably why the many observational studies of talk in the
classroom show first that teachers monopolise discussion and,
second, impose their definitions upon it (Delamont, 1983). This
imbalance is however difficult to evaluate. Those who see all
knowledge as relative might prefer 100 per cent negotiation of
meanings in the classroom, while those taking an absolute and
traditional view might favour 100 per cent transmission by the
teacher. But most would settle for a compromise. Some areas of
the curriculum seem so important and agreed as valuable that it
would penalise children not to teach them. Others are areas of
dispute or debate and should be open to negotiation. It is
probable that the balance is tilted towards teacher-dominated
interaction because genuine negotiation requires some abdication of authority. But both extremes need thinking through
before assuming that the many radical and reactionary advocates
have a cast-iron case. The liberal compromise, adopted by most
teachers once they think out their position, may be a fair
reflection of reality.

Language, Meanings and Social Backgrounds

The different meanings incorporated into language come from
different experiences, mostly outside, antedating the classroom.
This is obviously very important for teaching. No area has been
subject to so much attention in initial and in-service training of
teachers and yet so subject to both exampling, the gathering of
selected evidence to support theories, and to stretching that
evidence to apply those theories to practice. Furthermore, the
idea that the scope of our thinking is determined by the language
available to us is fascinating. It suggests that we are not merely
teaching children to read, write, talk and listen, but are

influencing their view of the world while they interpret our messages from their background. But it is safest to identify what seems to be dependable information in this seductive area before looking at the hunches and hypotheses.

The concrete base for looking at the social role of language in education is built of the following factors:

1   individuals from identifiable groups are likely to have differing social constructions of the reality they face;
2   teachers are rarely in a position where they can release their control over the definition of the valued and re- warded in the classroom;
3   the language used by individuals is influenced or de- termined by their social settings;
4   there are social class, ethnic and gender differences in attainment.

There is obviously some connection between these factors. Children of Fellows of the Royal Society are likely to see the world as theirs for the mastering; they are likely to fit easily into the language of school and to achieve more academically than children of the poor. But there will be exceptions. Whatever causes the differences on average is not all-pervasive, for the poor do succeed and the rich do fail. There is also a cautionary note in the words above. There are various social constructions of reality not just one, and individuals belong to many social settings that may contain very different interpretations of the world. Thus, it is grossly over-simplified to refer to teachers as having middle-class views. Many have working-class origins. They may be men or women. They will have minority interests. All are affected by prevailing social arrangements and assump- tions. Even as a group they show little consistency. They seem to vote conservative, yet support unions that belong to the Trades Union Congress. This warning about generalisation applies to all adults and to children. We are in a subject where only tentative explanations are possible.

In Britain the major influence in developing theories of the relation of language and social structure has been Bernstein. Since the early 1960s he has produced a flow of stimulating, if inconsistent, articles that have served as the basis of a secondary industry drawing out conclusions for education. Bernstein has also modified his views on language across the last twenty years. The industry declined in the 1970s having had the same rise and fall as many other theories developed in the human sciences, and applied to education without care for the gap between speculation plus exampling and stretching plus application.

The safest approach to Bernstein is to see him as essentially a sociologist searching for the forces that seem to underlie and account for social behaviour. Thus Atkinson (1981) argues that Bernstein is best considered as a structuralist, concerned less with surface phenomenon such as language, as with the structures that hold together diverse surface behaviour including language. Thus the term linguistic 'code' is best used as we use the model of genetic 'code', as a mechanism programming and regulating surface manifestations. Thus speech and perception are determined by the underlying code. This view avoids trivialising linguistic code into a superficial form of speaking. Bernstein is concerned with the social construction of meaning. Language plays a central part in this. But he is looking at its architecture rather than its application. The concern is with trying to understand what binds us together socially. Trying to apply Bernstein's work to education is difficult because his concern is with the theoretical rather than the practical.

My interpretation is that Bernstein's early theories proposed a *restricted* and an *elaborated* code (Bernstein, 1961). Middle-class children had access to both codes, but the working class to only the restricted code. Hence, as the language of schooling was elaborated, the working class were penalised and this could account for their low attainment. However, while there was plenty of evidence that there were social class differences in language (for example, Hawkins, 1969), even those who produced it now seem to accept that what really matters is the social context in which differences occur. It is possible that working-class children could use a very elaborated code in one context, but could still be restricted in the classroom (for example, Hawkins, 1977). Bernstein has also changed his interpretation of differences in language use to take in this point about language as always context-bound (Bernstein, 1973). Thus, children may use different degrees of elaboration in different contexts. Furthermore, in these later versions linguistic codes were given their underlying, structural definition (Bernstein, 1971). But as this reinterpretation occurred, the theory also became more complicated. Language, social class, family structure and mode of thinking are related. The search was for the underlying structures. These were seen to be 'positional' or 'person'-

centred family structures that promoted restricted, and/or elaborated, codes respectively.

The most striking feature of this shift of interpretation from a context-free theory of language use used by different social classes, to one stressing social contexts is that it moves the argument not only to a deeper sociological level, but away from differences fixed by social background to a conflict that can be resolved by teachers. If the conflict results from the language of the classroom, then that can be changed. The practical problem becomes the inability or unwillingness of teachers to acknowledge and value the language of children whose background promotes a complicated language, but not that used in the classroom. This can be illustrated by considering the 'deficit' model seen to be used by Bernstein in his early work, and by contrasting it with theories that acknowledge differences, but see these as constructed and thence man-made and manageable. Here working-class language is not deficient, just different in being rich in its own contexts.

Ironically Bernstein's most popular article, 'Education cannot compensate for society' (Bernstein, 1970), is an attack on the notion of compensatory education and the deficit model. This is seen as deflecting attention from what goes on in school to assumed problems in the home and the culture, hence removing the responsibility of teachers to tackle low attainment. This view is the opposite of the simple interpretations of Bernstein's early work that took the restricted code as a problem within the working class or among minority groups. If there was any misunderstanding about the weakness of this assumption of a single set of social class codes, it was clarified by the work of Labov in America (1969) and by writers such as Wight and Norris (1970) and Sinclair and Coulthard (1975) in England. Labov's point is simple but powerful, and is backed by research into language use in natural rather than experimental settings. Blacks in the US used a rich language in their own environment, but the mutual ignorance of teachers and children in inner city and other schools often led to the language of the latter seeming restricted. Labov's later work suggests that black communities actually value verbal fluency more highly than middle-class white cultures (Labov, 1972).

The social pathology model assuming language deprivation among the poor or among minority groups dominated education into the early 1970s. The search was for causes of the problem outside the school in family, community, minority language or culture. Starting with an assumption that there were deficiencies located in the family, home or culture, led to solutions being sought in compensation. The acknowledgment of rich but different languages has led to a new emphasis on the work of different dialects, on using these in school and helping children to develop their own strengths in their own words. This shift in the perspectives on language has been tellingly documented by Burton (1983) and has brought a more positive attitude to the language that children bring to school, and a concern that curriculum should not devalue their culture, but reflect its value.

It is difficult not to feel perplexed about the apparent contradictions in the sociological, socio-linguistic evidence. It is typical of the difficulties in using ideas developed to try to understand the foundations of human social behaviour to help inform practice in the classroom. Exampling and stretching are inevitable. Yet consideration of these ideas is essential if the evidence that is available on learning and teaching is to be understood. The tendency has been to ignore the active way that situations such as classrooms are interpreted. The emphasis on the tasks in hand and the characteristics of the children in determining the effectiveness of teaching leads inexorably to a consideration of how those tasks are perceived and related to the antecedent social experience of teachers and learners.

Sociological Perspectives and Human Learning

The sociological and socio-linguistic evidence on learning, like its psychological counterpart, is based in models of human behaviour. The same series of questions needs asking. Why are these recommendations for practice drawn from this evidence? What reliability and validity has it? What hunches or hypotheses directed the research? From what theoretical model were these derived? Why was this model chosen as a source rather than its competitors? How is that chosen model related to political and philosophical views on the nature of man and the structure of society? The answers will provide clues to the limitations and possibly the bias in the evidence. Clearly, these sociological questions are at a different level from those asked by psychologists. The concern is with underlying assumptions and the distribution of power that determines what is valued in education.

The consequence of the way definitions of what counts as valuable can be seen is the failure to motivate identifiable social groups. The average attainment of the unskilled working class, of black children and of girls may be depressed below that expected given their ability, by the content of the curriculum and the way it is taught.

Once the relationship between curriculum and attainment is examined, the 'why' and 'how' questions remain to be answered, just as they are when psychologists look at the mental processes in learning. There has been increased interest in the part played by the language used in the classroom as an important factor in determining relative attainment. But once again it is necessary to be cautious. The models, and the hypotheses derived from them, have been presented, built into advice for teachers and then quickly challenged. This suggests more speculation than a solid base for action.

NOTES

1 This chapter is not concerned with the learning of language, although the discussions about theoretical models and methods of enquiry apply to language as to other learning. Indeed, there is probably more than average conflict between supporters of different models over the way language is, or is best, learned. In particular the behaviourist approach stressing the role of trial and error, the use of rewards or corrections to reinforce correct and inhibit incorrect learning is still opposed to models stressing the way children develop spontaneously, the existence of inherited programmes for language acquisition and the importance of social interaction.

2 This is a difficult idea to grasp. It involves seeing classrooms and other scenes of social interaction as networks of meanings that may contrast and conflict and which have to be reconciled for effective learning to occur. Teachers and children are likely to hold very different interpretations of events in the school and of the curriculum. Among the children there will be a variety of views given their different social backgrounds. Thus knowledge, values, the curriculum and so on are not necessarily given and accepted in the form of syllabuses, textbooks, worksheets and teaching styles, but are interpreted by all those involved, drawing on different experiences to give meaning. Teaching from this view is rarely transmission from teacher to learner, but negotiation, through

which children not only impose their own interpretations on to the learning experience, but help to determine the way the work of a class proceeds and is evaluated.

3   This is illustrated in the Inner London Education Authority's initiative to encourage the staff of schools to examine the bases of low attainment in *Race, Sex and Class* (ILEA, 1983). The curriculum and the organisation of schools were to be examined to see if they contained approaches that could be seen as meaningless or demeaning by identifiable groups of children.

4   ORACLE, the Observational and Classroom Learning Evaluation project, is examined in Chapters 4 and 5. It is a major research project based at the University of Leicester looking at the organisation of learning in primary schools through the use of observation in classrooms (Galton, Simon and Croll, 1980; Galton and Simon, 1980; Simon and Willcocks, 1981; Galton and Willcocks, 1983).

4 From Teaching Models to Classroom Practice: Context and Content

Moving from considerations of models to practice in the classroom, the shift of emphasis is from the universal to the particular. Researchers seek general principles; teachers seek ways forward in their own classroom situation. This leaves an author with a problem. It is easy to detect that there is a wide gap between the intentions of teachers and the way these work out in practice or, as in this chapter, between models and practice. This involves judgements that are based either in research evidence, or the evidence that is real to teachers. As an example, Southgate used scores on standardised tests of reading to assess the accuracy of teachers' estimates of children's reading in the *Extending Beginning Reading* research (Southgate, Arnold and Johnson, 1981). But it has been pointed out that an alternative would have been to accept the validity of teacher assessments and to have used these to assess the value of the tests (Stierer, 1982). The criticisms of the teachers were based on an acceptance of the test scores. But knowing the weaknesses of such tests, why should they be taken as the criterion of performance and not the professional judgements of teachers who had known the children over a long period? That caution has to be remembered as we move into the classroom.

There are certain constraints on teaching that have to be considered before looking at the relation between theoretical perspectives of teaching and actual practice. The architecture of schools, the resources available, the external pressures to retain a basic curriculum, an authority structure, accountability and some decorum, the habits brought into the school by children and the support given by parents, all restrict the freedom of teachers in their choice of classroom organisation. Schools are context-bound. They receive widely differing inputs of resources and children. They are organised differently and achieve different combinations of attainments. But it is still realistic to generalise. What is remarkable about schools is not their differences but their similarity. This applies not only today, but across centuries. A teacher from a monitorial school would have little difficulty in a contemporary school classroom. For all the many revolutions and innovations, change has been slow.

This chapter is organised to give first a picture of the primary school classroom from the evidence available. This description is then followed in Chapter 5 by the evidence on the styles adopted by teachers and the way these are related to the organisation of the children for learning. These organisations are then related to the learning theories outlined in Chapter 2. Finally these practices in the classroom are related to various theories of primary education, particularly those recommended in the Plowden Report (DES, 1967).

It is inevitable that research into classroom practices will focus on gaps between intentions and practices. The motivation behind research, evaluation or inspection is to improve the learning situation and this means identifying areas of strength and weakness. This has to be remembered when reviewing the available evidence. The research is rarely planned to be a cosmetic or a hatchet job. But even description will tend to be concentrated where the results turn out to be eye-catching or unexpected or where improvement is obviously required. It is fair therefore to introduce the evidence on classrooms by stressing that the researchers in the ORACLE and other projects found the children well behaved, highly motivated, contented, busy and progressing in their work.

There is a rich variety of evidence available on classroom activity, including the relation between teaching and the response of pupils. First, there are surveys of the allocation of time and effort. The Observational and Classroom Learning Evaluation project (ORACLE) at the University of Leicester has been productive since funding in 1975 (see, for example, Galton, Simon and Croll, 1980; Galton and Simon, 1980; Simon and Willcocks, 1981). At the University of Lancaster there have been major studies under Bennett (see, for example, Bennett, 1976; Bennett et al., 1980, 1984). The Teacher Education project at the University of Nottingham also included classroom studies (Wragg, 1984). These have provided a wealth of information on the way the curriculum is organised and the way teachers and pupils spend their time. This information complements that in the three national surveys of primary, secondary and infant schools by HM Inspectors (DES, 1978; DES, 1979; DES, 1982). Other evidence is available in studies of the teaching of specific subject areas, particularly reading (for example, see Southgate *et al.*, 1981). There are also evaluations of the way learning is organised (for example, Barker-Lunn, 1970) and of the problems arising from curriculum developments (for example, Hamilton, 1975). Finally, there are studies of the interaction between teachers and pupils (for example, Stubbs and Delamont, 1976; McAleese and Hamilton, 1978; and Delamont, 1983).

The Design of Schools and the Relation between Pupils and Teachers

There is a combination of educational philosophy and financial consideration in the design of classroom and schools. Thus Seaborne (1971) gives the typical monitorial (Lancaster) classroom as accommodating about 320 children in a 70 by 32 foot space with rows of desks facing the teacher's platform, and space for monitors to move between the rows. This single classroom with one teacher in charge was modelled on the ancient grammar schools. Once schools grew to accommodate the spread of mass education, they were built on the Prussian model with classrooms off a central hall so that the headteacher could keep an eye on the rooms of the teacher-assistants. In the twentieth century the closed classroom became the norm. In the 1950s there was a switch to building open-plan primary schools. But Bennett *et al.* (1980) warn that in the open-plan schools surveyed, there was no guarantee that open design meant open or informal teaching. Indeed, many teachers in this study were working as if they were in conventional classrooms and had arranged their rooms accordingly.

There is a financial factor that has always been taken into account in school building. Fluctuations in the number of births in different periods often lead to crises over too few or too many schools. The monitorial schools were both cheap and in line with the educational and economic philosophy behind them. There may also have been some economy in the switch to open-plan schools in the 1950s. But in all schools, including the Victorian three-deckers that can still be found in large towns, views on how children learned influenced design. This also applies inside the classrooms.

The easiest way of illustrating this relation of educational philosophy and school design is to look at the classrooms of different historical periods. Getzels (1978) points to four school buildings near his office in Chicago to make an observation that could be made in most cities of the industrial world. In early twentieth century schools the teacher's desk is central, at the front and facing straight rows of desks. The 1930s design was for moveable chairs, with the teacher's desk in the corner. The 1950s classroom had trapezoidal desks capable of forming a circle. The 1970s school was open-plan with no teachers' or pupils' desks, but various spaces for diverse activities.

To Getzels these layouts in classrooms reflect different conceptions of learning. The straight lines of desks facing the teacher were to seat empty organisms learning by trial and error, all linked to the teacher by stimulus-response bonds. In the 1930s the individual child's needs were seen as paramount rather than any connection to the teacher. By the 1950s learning was seen as a social process, hence the need for a circle of desks. In the 1970s children were seen to be spontaneous in their interaction with the environment, hence the design allowing such spontaneity with little teacher visibility.

The importance of the confinement of learning in a school-room comes partly from the direct constraint this imposes on organisation. The emphasis on the maintenance of order in the classroom, for example, is obviously related to the problem of confining active children in a small space for hours on end. But even more important is that the teachers' perspectives of teaching seem to be affected by the classroom box. That does not only account for the minor changes in layout as theories of the way children learn change; it explains why open-plan schools often get divided up into classrooms by the use of bookshelves and cupboards. Teachers seem at home in a space with their children. So do the children. We might have the image of the self-contained classroom deeply engrained in our idea of the school. It is part of our mental construction of the proper, natural context for learning. In turn that idea limits attempts to organise learning more effectively. That possibility has to be remembered as a description of activity in the classroom is read. It could also be influential in accounting for teaching styles and the way learning is organised. The striking aspect of schools is not their differences but their similarity.

What is on the Timetable?

The Plowden Report gave an impression of rapid change in the primary school curriculum. The Black Papers, starting with Cox and Dyson in 1969 and continuing to the fifth volume in 1977 (Cox and Boyson, 1977) reinforced the impression of extensive innovation by criticising the switch from basic skills to child-centred activity in the curriculum. But research across this period and into the 1980s did not confirm any major change apart from the growth of mixed ability grouping. The emphasis on the three Rs looked as strong in the early 1980s as it did twenty years before (Simon, 1981). Teachers remained firmly in control of the curriculum in the classroom. It is the accumulation of evidence which now enables a convincing picture of what is on the timetable to be drawn. It suggests that there is considerable variety in the allocation of time to each of the basic skills, but that there has been no dramatic decrease in line with an extensive child-centred movement or a switch to integrated work.

Mathematics and language work tend to dominate the activities of the primary school classroom. Below are the ranges and average times spent on these skills as observed by various researchers.[1]

MATHEMATICS
ORACLE (Galton, Simon and Croll, 1980): Pupils were engaged for 33.1 per cent of their time on mathematics, consisting of 16.0 per cent on number work, 4.3 per cent on practical work and 10.2 per cent on abstract mathematics.
Bennett et al. *(1980):* An average of 17.1 per cent of all time-tabled time allocated, with a range of 9.2 up to 26.5 per cent.
Bassey (1978): The most frequent response from 900 junior school teachers was four and a quarter to five hours per week with a range from a quarter to one hour up to seven and a quarter to eight hours.

LANGUAGE
Bassey (1978): The most frequent responses for time spent on language work were between six and a quarter and eight hours

per week with a range of a quarter to one hour up to nine and a quarter to ten hours.

Bennett et al. *(1980):* An average of 30.7 per cent of all timetabled time allocated, with a range of 16.6 to 46.4 per cent.

ORACLE (Galton, Simon and Croll, 1980): Pupils were engaged 36.1 per cent on language work, consisting of 4.4 per cent reading, 21.2 per cent writing and 2.0 per cent spoken English.

Ashton(1975): Junior school headteachers reported time spent on language from three and three-quarter to thirteen and three-quarter hours per week.

The accumulated evidence of these studies suggest first that there has certainly not been any abandonment of work in the basic skills area. For example, Bennett (1976) reported that 80 per cent of primary teachers in the sample expected multiplication tables to be learned by heart. However, there remains a remarkable variety in the time allocated to mathematics and to language. This allocation should of course be interpreted with caution. Mathematics and language are part of many activities and it is difficult to quantify this indirect learning which is often most important as it shows how the basic skills are used in practice rather than as independent exercises.

The easiest area to identify after the basic skills is Aesthetics including music or art and craft. Bennett *et al.* (1980) report 10.3 per cent of time allocated to aesthetics with a range of 2.3 to 17.7 per cent. Bassey (1978) reports one and a quarter to two hours out of twenty-seven and a half per week for Art and Craft as the most popular time, with a range of a quarter to one up to four and a quarter to five hours. Galton, Simon and Croll (1980) give 10.3 per cent of time to Art and Craft. Once again the average time is similar but the ranges are great. This also applies to physical education. After that the studies are not comparable, because areas such as integrated studies, general studies and thematic studies tend to be defined differently by different researchers.

The picture that emerges from this timetabled activity is of a common core of work in the basic 'vehicle' subjects, but with wide variations in individual classrooms. Certainly there is no uniformity given the ranges indicated. But neither is there evidence of teachers abdicating their responsibility to organise a curriculum, to keep around half the time on aspects of mathematics and language and to provide a variety of 'tapestry' subjects. A comparison with the suggestions from the DES (1981) for a common core in the primary school shows the schools in the research samples roughly in line with official policy. But there is considerable individuality around this core and in the priorities within it. Not only is the allocation of time divergent, but the balance of work within each subject varies widely. Neither those concerned with a possible abdication of teacher responsibility for ensuring adequate cover in basic skills, nor teachers concerned with their professional freedom to determine their own classroom regime seem to have cause for panic.

What is the Pattern of the Working Day for Teachers?

The picture that comes from both observational and questionnaire studies of teachers in action is of a fragmented 'busyness'. The main source of evidence is Hilsum and Cane's *The Teacher's Day* (1971). While pupil–teacher ratios have fallen since then, it is unlikely that the picture is now very different, particularly as LEAs have cut back teaching staff in schools. The job is nothing like the stereotyped image of a combination of periods spent talking to the whole class, or of the class working quietly in groups or individually, while the teacher talks to children called to the front, or while circulating around the classroom. Indeed, the working day for teachers is continually fractured by demands that may have little to do with the organisation of learning.

First, Hilsum and Cane found a long working day of over eight hours of which only a quarter was spent in teaching. Over 40 per cent of the work was outside the classroom, consulting, planning, marking, supervising and so on. Even within the classroom during teaching sessions, under half the time was spent in teaching. Thirty-five per cent of time was devoted to organising work, general supervision, and clerical and mechanical tasks. Much of this work was routine but time-consuming maintenance. Teachers were sharpening pencils, cutting up paper, setting up apparatus, tidying up the room, marking registers, completing dinner lists, filling up forms.

Much of the preparation and maintenance took teachers out of their classrooms. Even in peak times they were on the move. In their contact time with children they sat for a third of the time, but got up and sat down 30 times a day in the classroom. Playground supervision, checking children in corridors, taking games, dance, nature rambles, meant further activity. Long, peaceful, still periods either with a class or relaxing at lunch time, were rare. Furthermore, in the classroom one job was being done while other demands were mounting and becoming urgent. Listening to a child read was accompanied by awareness of disturbance over there. Children were waiting outside the staffroom, despite the prohibition, while coffee was being drunk. Parents were talked to while the playground had to be supervised. At all times eyes were needed in the back of the head and periods of concentration were short.

The most remarkable feature of the Hilsum and Cane study, as well as others, was this fragmented nature of the teacher's day. For example, there was an average of 123 minutes of lesson instruction per day. But this was broken up into 117 instances. There were no long uninterrupted sequences of teaching. The 44 minutes of organising were spread across 40 occasions and the four minutes on 'discipline' were also spread across 40 occasions, meaning a hasty word rather than any sustained action. There were two minutes described as 'pastoral' work during the day. This seems surprisingly little considering the importance of this guidance and help for individual children. But it was also spread across eight instances, giving a norm of 15 seconds.[2]

This evidence of a day broken up into many different activities, each lasting a brief period, is confirmed in other research. Southgate et al. (1981) sees teachers driving themselves hard to extend beginning reading. They had a high 'task-orientation'. However, during the 20 minute periods observed in this study the average number of switches of attention by the teacher was 15. Similarly in the ORACLE project 'busyness' was the outstanding feature of the teachers and children observed (Galton, Simon and Croll, 1980). Yet in general the classrooms were orderly, the work largely done individually by the pupils, and the teacher was not only in control, but was 'all-pervasive'. In one of the four categories of teacher identified, the 'individual monitors' containing 22.4 per cent of the sample of teachers, the strategy chosen of organising and monitoring individual pupil work inevitably put them under pressure. But even in the most formal group, the 'class enquirers', much time was spent moving around among the children asking questions and giving answers.

Thus 'busyness' and fragmentation emerge from research based on observation of classrooms as the closest descriptions of the teacher's day. The day is broken up by the interruptions necessitated by tasks involved in managing the school. But even more important are the unpredictable actions of 30 or so young children confined in a classroom. The teachers were in charge, but interactions with pupils were short-lived because the teachers were keeping the momentum going by a series of brief instructions, corrections or movements to individuals, groups and the whole class. In the ORACLE classrooms for example, disruptive behaviour by children was rare. Despite the rush and bustle classroom management seemed effective. But all the researchers queried the effectiveness of the organisation of learning in these conditions. That is the subject of Chapter 5.

Pupil Involvement in Work

The amount of time allocated to a subject or in which children are observed to be engaged is only one aspect of their involvement. The advantage of observational studies of classrooms is that they give a picture of children at work or idling. In the ORACLE project researchers observed previously selected pupils at fixed intervals, recording activity on to a schedule of activities. These researchers were trained and their observations were controlled, both in the time intervals and where they were to be looking. Hence studies such as ORACLE (for example Galton, Simon and Croll, 1980) and Bennett et al. (1980 and 1984) provide information that is often not available to teachers whose concern has to be with events as they arise rather than with pre-selected areas of the classroom at times given to the researcher.

It is, however, necessary to insert a caution. There is convincing American evidence that time spent on a task is an important factor in determining attainment (Wiley and Harnischfeger, 1974). Bennett (1979) gives it a central place in his model of effective teaching. But time off the task is often very productive, particularly, in extending thinking beyond the mechanical. This was the message in the evidence from Armstrong (1980), quoted in Chapter 2 (pages 31–2). Second, children differ widely in their working habits, as do adults. The

ORACLE project's 'solitary workers' may benefit from a very different time-on-task from the 'intermittent workers'. Finally, controlled observation can detect whether a child is writing or reading or even looking as if he or she is thinking, but cannot detect the thought behind the industry observed, what is going on in the mind of the dreamer, or the value of the talking in the chattering group. It is wise not to be too puritanical in recommending maximum time-on-task, while still accepting it as an essential factor in successful and sustained learning.

Bennett *et al.* (1980), investigating open-plan schools, provide the most comprehensive statistical account of pupil involvement. For juniors involved in language work, the time actually engaged was 69.7 per cent with a range of 50 to 85 per cent. In mathematics, average involvement was 67.9 per cent, with a range of 60 to 90 per cent. Average involvement for all curricular activities was 76.2 per cent. However, not all the time in the classroom is spent on language, mathematics, environmental studies and so on. In all the 12 open-plan units studied, 13.0 per cent of the time was spent on administration and transition and another 20.6 per cent spent in non-involvement. Thus pupils were involved in curricular activities for 66.4 per cent of the time available.

This figure of around two-thirds involvement by juniors in their work recurs in many studies. In *Extending Beginning Reading*, Southgate's (1981) team collected 224 observation schedules on children showing one-third non-task-directed, diversionary activity. This tended to increase towards the end of the time allocated for the task. The teachers concentrated on hearing individual children read, thus leaving many others to divert themselves. The range of time-on-task by pupils varied from 100 per cent down to 12 per cent. In the ORACLE classrooms children were found to be fully involved on task for 58 per cent of their time, but another 12 per cent was spent in preparing and maintaining the work such as sharpening pencils (Galton and Simon, 1980).

More evidence can be found in observations of individual children. Bennett (1980) presents case studies in open-plan junior classrooms. The curriculum followed by Jane and Tracey was similar in the allocation of time to subjects. But the level of their involvement differed widely. Jane's overall involvement was 71 per cent in a unit with an average of 69.2 compared with the average for all the units studied of 52.3. But Tracey, in a unit with an average involvement of only 35.1 per cent, attained only 27.1 per cent herself.

Behind these figures lies the variety facing teachers. Jane was in a suburban school in the South of England. Teachers met daily to discuss pupil progress. They could allow freedom and self-direction in learning. Staffing was generous and 'waiting for teacher's attention', a common source of non-involvement, was rare, accounting for only 1.5 per cent of Jane's time. Tracey was in a school serving a mixed catchment area with a staff described as resistant to the open-plan building. The involvement of all children was low and the time spent in administration and transition was high. Much of Tracey's time while not working was taken up with chattering and fidgeting. Bennett sees this as possibly connected with teaching methods that were not appropriate to the way work was organised. Tracey is described as from the lower ability range of the school. In a situation where children such as Tracey work individually for long periods of the day, yet the work is essentially teacher directed, it looks as if the teaching is at fault. Contacts with teachers were few. Tracey idled most of the day away. But it is difficult to sort out cause and effect. What seemed necessary was to change the organisation to narrow some of the gap between the whole class teaching that predominated and the scope for individual children to drift along without attention.

Again it has to be stressed that not working may be productive. In the ORACLE classrooms a negligible amount of time was spent on disruptive activity and the researchers' emphasis on the 'busyness' observed does not suggest idleness. Two aspects are worrying, however. First, there was a wide range of industry and idleness among the children. The case studies of children suggest that, in extreme cases, patterns of work were being fixed very early in the primary schools and that this could account for the increasing differences between the attainment of different groups later on. Second, while it would be absurd to view classrooms as conveyor belt factories in which children should be working flat-out all the time, evidence from the various research projects is of a gap between the teacher's perception of children's work and the patterns observed. This may lead to a neglect of the formation of harmful working habits among identifiable groups of children, thus reducing the effectiveness of any remedial action taken later.

The Effectiveness of Teaching

It seems obvious that the characteristics of an effective teacher can be observed and therefore defined. There is a sequence, a structure of events that can promote learning. Regardless of the model selected, there is a syntax in learning that needs organisation. That does not however lead directly to a model for teaching. The strategies adopted by teachers will differ according to their personal values, their strengths and weaknesses as communicators or organisers and the situations they face. It may be promising to look for the characteristics of the effective teacher. The problems however are immense. Not only teachers, but the children for whom they are responsible, have an individuality that makes generalisation perilous. The environments for teaching also vary. The search for the effective teaching style is important, but it starts neither with a single learning model nor a uniform context for that learning.

The first step in the search for clues to effective teaching is to acknowledge the importance of organisation. This applies not only to any model of learning used as a theoretical basis, but to the conditions in the classrooms. Studies of successful 'informal' teachers who maximise the opportunities for children to take responsibility for their own learning show planning and a high work rate on the job as key features (see, for example, Wragg, 1978).[3] Studies of changes in the primary school classroom since the Plowden Report in 1967 confirm that there has been no relaxation of the control exercised. Whether classrooms were formally or informally organised the teacher remained firmly in control (see, for example, Simon, 1981).

The persistence of firm organisation by teachers, even when their aim may have been to maximise the opportunities for children to learn for themselves, follows from the models of learning available and the conditions for their implementation. Teachers can still exercise their control in very different ways. The spectrum of approaches from teachers ranges from emphasising the capacity of children to seek actively, find, and master the knowledge necessary to fulfil themselves at one extreme, to stressing the responsibility of teachers to ensure that all children progress through a basic curriculum at the other. There are many contrasting approaches to effectiveness. Each combines beliefs and perspectives at different levels. First there is the philosophical level where the nature of children is debated. If this is seen as good and active, the structure required will be to give scope for unfolding of capacity. If it is seen as potentially evil, it will lead to a drive to affect salvation through discipline. If it is seen as neutral, or as good but inactive, it will lead to seeing teaching as initiating and controlling the learning action.[4]

The second level is more practical. Even the most optimistic beliefs about children will not eliminate the need to protect them from dangers or to introduce them to some essential learning early in life. Rousseau is usually seen as the philosopher most responsible for the modern view of man as naturally good, perverted by unjust social arrangements and of the need to let children grow naturally. But he sent his own children off to an orphanage. The most progressive mother in Islington would be culpable if she did not curb her child's urge to play in the middle of Highbury Corner during the rush hour. None of the developments in the primary school seems to have weakened teachers' concentration on ensuring that basic skills are taught early in a child's school career.

The third level is the variety among children and teachers, in the interaction in and around the classroom. There is no best way of teaching because children are persons in their own right before they arrive at school. They bring their own experiences, values and bases for interpreting schooling. So do teachers. Furthermore, each engages actively in the interaction in the classroom as elsewhere. Parents do not bring up passive offspring, they learn from them as they try to guide. Similarly, teachers do not just transmit knowledge, values and skills, they learn to adapt by observing and listening to the children. That, plus the range of different activities in the classroom, accounts for the many different approaches to teaching that may, at different times and for different purposes, be effective. The teaching style adopted may affect the responses of the children. It is always assumed that it does, even if the evidence is less than completely convincing (see, for example, Elashoff and Snow, 1971). But there is also evidence that suggests that teachers do adjust to responses of children (see, for example, Jackson and Belford, 1965). This interaction adds to the need for caution over recommendations to adopt any particular approach to teaching. It is unlikely that any one style will suit all teachers, all children, in all classrooms, at all times. As with learning theories it is more likely that a repertoire of styles will prove more useful.

The translation of models of learning into recommendations for teaching has not been easy. Nearly two hundred years after Pestalozzi, we are still looking for optimum methods based on a firm basis in evidence. The common elements in the various learning theories identified at the end of Chapter 2 (pages 26–32) are not easy to extract and have not been adopted as routine by teachers. The problem is not just that the evidence is conflicting and that the models are concerned with different tasks and opposed approaches. There is also a danger in each extreme. A top-down approach to the organisation of learning is liable to leave a lot of children, particularly if young, unable to understand, failing to master the concepts. This might be less of a problem if the relation between task and the age and abilities of the children was always carefully considered. It might be alleviated if time were given for each child to achieve mastery at his or her own pace. But teaching is usually organised to move all children on at a similar speed. The danger in this is not just a lot of frustration for learner and teacher, but the likelihood of the latter looking for the cause of the problem in the child. Most of the causes of low attainment in the literature connected with intelligence, personality, motivation, social or cultural background tend to be defined as beyond the teacher's control. We are back in the determinist trap discussed in Chapter 1.

The bottom-up approaches avoid slipping into placing the cause within the child or in some social situation in the child's past. By concentrating on current behaviour, improvements can be organised by setting realistic, attainable objectives. The work can be based on an analysis of the child's current attainments. Reinforcement can be planned and support gathered from the home. In other words, all the contingencies that can aid learning can be actively managed by the teacher. The problem here is that while such highly structured teaching seems to be effective for teaching basic skills and in behaviour modification, it is limited in its scope and often objectionable in the control that has to be exercised. Many important skills, the application of acquired knowledge and the imaginative development of attitudes in children seem to require an open-ended organisation to allow scope for active, insightful learning.

These extreme cases and their strengths and weaknesses point to the way learning theories can beneficially influence teaching. They tend to confirm that no one model, no one approach, is going to be optimal in all situations. Operant conditioning with its emphasis on reinforcement following the learning, is a powerful way of modifying behaviour and teaching skills systematically. At the other extreme, advanced organisers, designed to prepare children to think through the conceptual structure of subject matter when it is presented, can promote active, generalising learning. Joyce and Weil's view that a repertoire of models should be learned by teachers to match tasks in hand seems appropriate. Behind that view is a recognition that different learning theories contain important messages for teachers. It is frustrating looking for these among the conflict. But that conflict is often the consequence of investigating the learning of very different tasks and of concentrating on very different aspects of human learning. Generally the simpler tasks have involved behavioural approaches that are themselves simplified by concentrating on current behaviour, not the past history of those involved or aspects in their minds. On the other hand, conceptualising has usually been seen to be mainly concerned with more complicated tasks and more problematic situations. A hungry rat learning to press a lever to get food is taught by rewarding this action. There is no need to consider its personality, intelligence or family life in the cage. A child trying to envisage what life was like among Stone Age people is processing complicated information. Past experience and accumulated knowledge are going to be very important. In both cases there is common ground in the need to organise the learning situation, provide the materials, the clues and cues, prepare and motivate the learner for the task and ensure that it is at a level where success is likely. Finally, both extremes of learning depend on reinforcement. The rat is no doubt encouraged by receiving a pellet of food. The child is encouraged by a word of praise. In both cases the sooner this comes after successful performance, the more encouraging it will be. But the organisation has to go beyond reinforcing the immediate learning to extend and generalise it.

The view discussed in this chapter has profound implications for teaching. The choice of different models of learning to match tasks or the characteristics of the learners contrasts with the search for consistent, stable teaching styles. Indeed, the idea of a teacher adopting and sticking to such a style, regardless of the job in hand, or the children to be taught, is difficult to understand. Yet it is just this search for consistent teaching styles and for their relation to pupil attainment that has exercised educational researchers. As the focus switches to studies within primary school classrooms, the contrast between the approaches to the study of teaching has to be remembered. One stresses stability in style, the other flexibility in matching means to ends.

NOTES

1   These figures are averages, but should be treated as approximations only. It is very difficult for researchers to assess how much mathematics or language work has actually been done. Each area of learning can be going on in a variety of activities not necessarily or specifically concerned with mathematics or language.

2   This is another reason for allowing a wide tolerance in figures reported in classroom observation studies. The 'busyness' of classrooms makes the quantification of activities very difficult. They tend to be confusing, particularly to outsiders.

3   There is nothing very surprising about these results. If teachers are efficient planners with a high work rate in the classroom it is likely that they would make any style work. Conversely, it is highly unlikely that even the most miraculous model would work with an inefficient and idle teacher. The necessity of organisation for informal as well as formal teaching increases the importance of hard work before, during and after the learning itself. The crucial questions, never answered because it would involve researchers in assessing the competence of the teachers observed, are 'do particular teaching styles attract efficient or inefficient teachers?' and 'are any styles proof against incompetence or particularly rewarding for the competent?'

4   These views are related to very different philosophies of childhood. The romantic view seeing children as basically good leads to recommendations for freeing them to develop naturally through play, free activity and enquiry. The view that children are born with original sin leads to recommendations that they be saved as quickly and effectively as possible, particularly if infant mortality rates are high. Leaving children to unfold would risk their damnation in hell. In a more agnostic present the organisation of active learning becomes an alternative, even if a compromise between organising for unforced development and imposing a tightly scheduled programme to ensure early salvation.

5 From Teaching Models to Teaching Practice: Processes

There is now a lot of evidence on the way teachers adopt distinctive styles in the classroom and put these into operation in the organisation for learning. This comes from both questionnaire and observational studies. Once again, the methods used tend to determine the evidence produced. Thus Bennett's dependence on questionnaire evidence in *Teaching Styles and Pupil Progress* (Bennett, 1976), although backed by observation, tends to ignore the processes, the activity within actual classrooms. Teachers were categorised on the basis of their response to questions about education in general. Not only may this not reflect their actual behaviour in the classroom, but it neglects the interaction with children that is likely to modify and complicate the style in practice. Observational studies are concentrated on processes. But the evidence presented is the interpretation of the researchers and may not reflect how the teachers observed interpreted their actions. Both approaches neglect the requirements of different learning tasks and the background influences on the perceptions of the children.

Teaching Styles

The most common categorisation of teaching styles is into formal and informal. Barker-Lunn (1970), for example, clustered the 72 teachers in her *Streaming in the Primary School* on the basis of responses to a questionnaire to produce a formal and an informal cluster. Similarly, Bennett (1976) identified three types, formal, mixed and informal. Bennett's initial cluster analysis established 12 teacher types which were later collapsed to three, for assessing impact on pupil progress. The 12 teachers in each of the three groups were selected because their individual profiles matched most closely that of the group.[1]

The formal-informal grouping is a crude way of categorising the many-sided activities of teachers. Nevertheless there do seem to be clusters of teachers at each end of the spectrum when questionnaire answers are analysed. However, it is not only the crudity of the two extreme groups that is a problem. There is no guarantee that answers to a questionnaire reflect accurately behaviour while in front of a class. This may itself be inconsistent. It may also be beneficially and intentionally adjusted to different tasks or different groups of children. In the ORACLE project the categorisation of teacher styles was based on observations in the classroom (Galton, Simon and Croll, 1980). It produced the four categories that follow. But there is no suggestion in the books on the ORACLE project that the teachers adopted different learning models to help children tackle different tasks. Indeed, much of the evidence in this and other research suggests that means chosen were often inappropriate for the end in view.

The ORACLE project involved observation in 19 primary schools in three LEAs. The teachers and pupils in these schools were studied over three years. The aim was to describe the typical features of the 58 teachers in the classrooms involved. The four groups into which the teachers were categorised are described below.

Individual monitors: Thirteen teachers fell into this group. These are didactic teachers, telling children what to do as individuals rather than as a class. Their interaction with individual children is largely through marking and correcting work. They are individual monitors because their favoured way of organising learning is through instructing individuals.

Class enquirers: The nine teachers in this group taught the class as a whole but also gave attention to individual pupils for 42.5 per cent of their time, although this was the lowest of the four types. The distinguishing feature of their style was an emphasis on asking questions, exploring ideas as well as asking for facts. The cognitive level expected by this group was the highest among the four groups.

Group instructors: The seven teachers in this category organised children into groups and arranged the work in detail. They concentrated on facts rather than ideas. However, even if their distinguishing feature was grouping, the children still spent less than 20 per cent of their time working in groups. Individual work remained the largest category as with all other types of organisation.

Style changers: The 29 teachers in this final group were divided further; they employed a mixture of the methods used by all teachers. The six *infrequent changers* changed their style of teaching deliberately during the year in an attempt to adjust to the progress of the children. Thus a class enquirer style could be altered to individual monitoring once the children had acquired the necessary skills for working independently. The nine *rotating changers* organised their classes into groups which were moved from one curriculum activity to the next during the day. Thus there would be a lot of re-organisation at switching times. The 14 *habitual changers* also changed activities during the day, but in an unplanned way. Thus class teaching could be adopted as a response to children getting restless during individual or group work.

The obvious question about these categories is 'how consistent were they over a period of time?' The follow-up by the ORACLE team suggested that teachers were stable in the styles they adopted. They also compared the organisation of the individual monitors with the most informal of Bennett's 12 groups, and their class enquirers with the most formal (Galton, Simon and Croll, 1980, pages 138–41). The differences between the extremes were less in the ORACLE results. Indeed, the ORACLE team suggest that all of their teachers would have fallen into Bennett's mixed group. This may be the result of the use of observation in one study and questionnaire in the other. To the ORACLE team this suggests that the formal–informal, traditional–progressive distinctions are not often found in practice.

Teaching Styles and the Organisation of Learning

The most dramatic finding of the ORACLE research was the extent of individual activity among children. Galton describes the time the children spend completing worksheets and writing exercises, particularly in the basic skills, as 'isolation'. The children worked as individuals for two-thirds of the time. This isolation means, firstly, that contacts with the teacher were rare, with the average contact time per week being four hours. However, only 35 minutes of this was individual attention. Another 22 minutes of attention came whilst in a group and the remaining three hours were spent listening to class teaching. This isolation from the teacher occurred in all teaching styles and confirms the findings from other classroom research.

The limited time spent by any child in contact with the teacher on an individual basis is a consequence of the logistics of the school class. One teacher with 30 children and all the administrative tasks reported in Chapter 4 (pages 54–6) can afford little time with individuals. Furthermore, the ORACLE team confirm what every teacher knows, that while dealing with one child, the others have to be occupied. Secondly, the attention-seekers in the class will be wanting either reassurance that they are doing well or, more likely, will be at the centre of any disturbance. The presence of these disturbers is likely to be the reason why the amount of genuine work in groups is minimal. It affords the troublesome too many opportunities for moving around to disturb others. As a result, individual contact between pupils and the teacher is not only limited, but also of a limited duration. In infant classes, Resnick (1972) reported a series of very brief interactions. This was also the pattern in the ORACLE junior classrooms and in the infant classrooms observed by King (1978) where the average time given to hearing individual children read was 73, often interrupted, seconds.

The first post-Plowden evidence on the difficulty in individualising work in the primary school classroom came from Bealing (1972). This study of 189 teachers showed the popularity of grouping as a way of organising work. It showed that there was a tight control over the action by teachers. It also showed the overwhelming emphasis on individual work, particularly in the basic subjects of reading, English and mathematics. In further articles (Boydell, 1974, 1975) limited contacts between teachers and pupils were reported. Private individual work dominated and contacts with teachers were not only fleeting, but mainly concerned with the supervision of tasks, rather than with any high level cognitive interchange.

The most detailed study of the attempt to individualise teaching comes from Southgate et al. (1981). This study is based on daily logs of activities kept by the teachers, as well as observations of them in action. The teachers gave between 20 and 100 minutes per day to children's reading. They organised this by listening to each child read. Yet the norm was for this to be a two to three minute stretch at a time. The average time of total concentration on the oral reading of any child was 30 seconds. In each 20 minute period a teacher would, on average, switch attention 32 times. Even without this distraction the amount of time available for individual children would be limited. If 20 minutes per day were devoted to hearing children reading, each in a class of thirty would each get an average of three minutes per week and at the maximum of 100 minutes per day, 17 minutes a week. Southgate justly asks why this individualised approach seems to have been accepted universally as the optimum method for extending reading skills. Some class or group teaching would have increased the teacher's influence and freed more time for the children to get on with their own reading. Much of their time seems to have been spent queueing to get to the teacher, or waiting to join such a queue, or for further instructions on what to do because the teacher was too busy trying to hear others read to organise the work of the rest of the class.

Southgate's questions about the stress on individualisation of learning would apply to the evidence presented in the ORACLE study. The classroom manifested 'busyness', but the organisation of learning seems to have reduced not only the time spent on work, but its intellectual level. Repetitive filling-in of worksheets, routine exercises and reading books that neither stretched nor interested, seemed to be the consequence of having to organise children to keep them busy in order to spare time for attention to individuals. This can never result in a satisfactory level of interaction in a busy classroom. Indeed, the ORACLE finding, that the children who did better than expected were the solitary workers who had little contact with either the teacher or other pupils, suggests that some children do not need individual attention to master basic skills. Many, of course, get this at home rather than at school. The premium given to one-to-one contact is difficult to justify in practice.

Pupil Responses and Teacher Styles

Within their classrooms the teachers taking part in the ORACLE project remained firmly in control. The children remained busy. The teachers moved around the room or talked to children coming up to their desks. In the classrooms observed, the weaker pupils received slightly more individual help, but boys and girls, children of different ages and of different social classes seemed to receive roughly equal attention by the teachers. How then did the children respond? The ORACLE team produced a fourfold categorisation of pupils based on systematic observation in the classroom.[2]

Attention seekers, comprising 20 per cent of the sample, fell into two categories. The first wanted constant feedback from the teacher and followed him or her around or waited beside the desk. The second group were sought out by the teacher because they were liable to disturb others or ostentatiously to be idle. *Intermittent workers*, comprising 36 per cent of the sample, avoided the teacher, but spent a lot of time chatting with other children. They had the lowest level of interaction with the teacher but the highest level with peers. Indeed, they seemed to avoid contact with the teacher in direct contrast to the attention seekers, yet they still spent two-thirds of their time on the task set.
Solitary workers, comprising 33 per cent of the sample, received little individual attention from the teacher or other pupils. They spent three-quarters of their time on the tasks set. They tended to remain in their place and to be single-minded in working, undeflected by their environment. They scored highest of all four categories of pupils on the tests of mathematics, reading and language. The ORACLE team saw this success as being achieved at the price of a loss in communication with the children's peers, although this could have been compensated for outside the classroom.
Quiet collaborators, comprising 12 per cent of the sample, were also industrious, but interacted with the teacher mainly as part of the group or the class. They tended to wait for the teacher's support rather than search for their own solutions to problems, or seek out the teacher as an individual.

The obvious question facing the ORACLE team was whether these categories of pupils were formed by the strategies adopted by the teachers. Alternative explanations could be that there was no influence of teaching style on pupil category, or that the working habits of the pupils influenced the teaching methods. Relating two very complicated sets of information about teachers and children is not easy and it is safest to remain sceptical and depend on only the big differences.

The most striking feature of the ORACLE evidence is the distribution of the intermittent workers whose work habits were erratic. The individual monitors, emphasising contacts with children rather than groups or the whole class, had nearly 50 per cent of intermittent workers in their class. The class enquirers, the form teachers, had only nine per cent. Whole class teaching seemed to cut down the opportunities for idling and distraction. This teaching style produced a majority of solitary workers. The rotating changers also produced 45 per cent of intermittent workers. Once again a style which fragmented the teacher's attention seemed to allow more intermittent working.

There was also a strikingly different distribution of solitary workers among the categories of teaching: the 65 per cent among classes of class enquirers compares with the 25, 23 and 21 per cent among group instructors, rotating changers and habitual changers respectively. The three latter styles also produced large proportions of intermittent workers. Thus there seems to be an apparently dramatic effect on the responses of pupils from the adoption of a distinct teaching style by the teacher. It is, however, unwise to be dogmatic about effective styles. Solitary workers may be productive, but this was observed to be at often routine, repetitive, even unthinking work and at the cost of communication with others. Intermittent working has its benefits and the time these children spent working still remained high at around two-thirds of their time. Group instructors produced a larger proportion of quiet collaborators than any other teaching style, but while their passivity might be a worry, many teachers would see this as a minor concern. Schools are organised on the assumption that children will stay reasonably subdued physically and in the hope that this will be accompanied by intellectual enterprise.

The ORACLE team are rightly cautious in producing reasons for the different pupil responses produced by different teaching styles. Class teaching may reduce opportunities for distraction and encourage solitary working. Rotation of groups may produce a lot of idling time. Group instruction may cut down solitary working and encourage quiet collaboration. But the important point is that there is an influence at all. If the teaching and pupil categories are at all stable, it is an important confirmation of a popular belief. The ORACLE team, through their replication of classroom observations, suggest that there is such stability. Hence it looks as if teachers have an important influence over pupil working habits. This suggests that the choice of learning theories and of models of teaching, which lie behind a consistent teaching strategy, are going to have a possibly lasting impact on the way children set about working, respond to tasks set and collaborate with their peers and with adults. But that raises a problem. Teaching styles may be consistent, but the learning in classrooms is diverse. The relation of style to classroom learning theories and the organisation of learning has to be clarified.

Teaching Model and the Organisation of Learning

The ORACLE team distinguish between teaching strategies and tactics. The former are seen as ways by which teachers translate their aims into action. They are concerned therefore with organising learning so that time wasted is kept to a minimum. Teaching tactics are short-term adjustments made to check behaviour and keep the class working minute by minute. But teaching strategies are usually taken to be more than consistently adopting class inquiry or individual monitoring or group instruction as a style. They include choice of curriculum, instruction and evaluation.

It is difficult to relate the teaching styles which seem to incorporate both strategies and tactics to any models of teaching based on specific learning theories. There was however one exception to this. The ORACLE team take the recommendations of the Plowden Committee that the child 'is the agent in his own learning' and relate the data presented to this Piaget-based learning model.[3] There is also data that relates indirectly to models of teaching, particularly the use of group work, of projects and the cognitive level of teacher–pupil interaction. However, while rejecting the usefulness of looking for a 'best' teaching style, and criticising Bennett (1976) for using crude, questionnaire-based categories, the ORACLE team also seem to be categorising as if teaching and the response of pupils were extracted from both the task in hand and the characteristics of the children. Yet throughout Chapters 2 and 3 these were stressed as the key factors in the choice of appropriate organisations for learning.

The crucial question for organising learning is 'What is the best way for these children to learn this task?' This emphasis on both children and task is implicit in all teaching and preparation for teaching. Indeed, one important reason why learning theories are difficult to adapt into teaching methods is that the individual differences among the school class not only make generalisation about methods difficult, but mean that each child is likely to interpret not only the actions of the teacher, but also the content of the learning in ways determined by factors outside the school in the history of each child. This is the subject of Chapter 6. Equally important, these factors will affect the way the task is conceived.

The missing factor in most studies of classroom action is the nature of the work going on. The ORACLE team justly criticise Bennett for relying on the informal–formal continuum. But the four ORACLE teaching styles and the pupil responses are also free of the context of the task in hand. Similarly, Bennett (1979) places heavy emphasis on the importance of time-on-task. The ORACLE evidence does not support this as the crucial factor in learning. But this evidence is unrelated to the work being done. Yet the work has such a range of complexity, content, depth and so on, that any suggestion of an optimum teaching style or stable relations between these and pupil responses seems odd. At any one time in a primary school classroom, the variety is likely to require very different organisations for maximum effectiveness.

The complexity of tasks can be seen by first considering the focus of the work. It may be concerned with knowledge, attitudes or skills. Each of these may involve work ranging from simple to complex. Thus it is not just that each subject area has different requirements for learning, but that within each there are many contrasting ends and possible means for attaining them. Thus a lesson on science may be concerned with learning simple facts about plants, or with generalisation about the distinguishing features of living things. It may be aimed at teaching children to be orderly when handling test-tubes, or be concerned to promote an attitude of sceptical questioning towards the material world. The teacher may be trying to get children to group into animal, vegetable or mineral, but the objective may also be to help children generate hypotheses from theories. All these, ranging from simple to complex, can be seen in any primary school classroom or any book on elementary science. Each requires a very different approach to the organisation of learning. No single teaching approach could effectively cover the lot.

The Quality of Learning in the Classroom

The study of sixteen able teachers and their classrooms by Bennett *et al.* (1984) has provided evidence on the planning of learning by teachers, the match between this and the abilities of the six- and seven- year-olds studied, and the way these children actually went about their work. The teachers were convinced of the value of individual work. They were dedicated and conscientious. But the focus on the planning of work and its implementation by children inevitably uncovered the gaps between aim and practice. These were apparent in three related areas, the organisation of the work, its relation to the capacities of the children and their facility for doing it their way.

The actual tasks set children were categorised by Bennett *et al.* as incremental (introducing new ideas), restructuring (demanding that children discover ideas for themselves), enrichment (using old skills on new problems), practice and, finally, revision. In language teaching, 76 per cent of tasks were practice; in number teaching, 43 per cent. Overall, only 7 per cent of tasks were either restructuring or enrichment, and 25 per cent were incremental. Across the sixteen classrooms there were wide variations. In one there were no incremental tasks observed, only practice and revision. In other classrooms over a third of tasks seen was new work. The choice of tasks always depends on the gradations in the subject matter, the time in a sequence of learning when observations were made, and the speed at which children are judged to be able to take on new work.

What was surprising in these observations of tasks set was the gap between the intention of the teacher and the actual demands made on the pupils.[4] The task design was often faulty. Practice tasks were designed and implemented successfully. But with incremental tasks teachers found it difficult to stop children converting them into practice. The problem lay in the design and the mis-diagnosis of the capacities of the children. In number teaching, 30 per cent of tasks did not result in children doing the type of work intended; in language, 20 per cent. This problem affected high attaining children in particular, where the teachers tended to underestimate their knowledge of concepts and skills in language and to both over- and underestimate this knowledge in number work.

Overall, more than half of the observed tasks were mismatched. Higher attainers tended to be underestimated, low attainers overestimated. This was seen as lost opportunities for the former, confusion for the latter. The teachers were aware of the tendency to overestimate the capacity of children, but no task was seen as too easy for a child. The consequence for the children was that the low attainers worked slowly and intermittently, making persistent demands on the teacher's time and spending time in queues. In contrast, the children whose capacity was underestimated worked diligently, but often churned out work that was unimaginative and below their potential. They were happy doing this, manifesting no lack of interest even though they classified over three-quarters of tasks as easy.

These difficulties with children at both ends of the ability spectrum were similar to those found among mixed ability first year classes in comprehensive schools studied in the Teacher Education Project. Kerry and Sands (1984) found that slow and bright pupils demonstrated similar symptoms of boredom, finishing work prematurely, lacking motivation and behaving disruptively. The teachers reported the problems in matching set work to ability and expressed their frustration at not being able to deal with them. Again it was with the bright pupils that teachers felt less able to detect problems and to cope with them. Yet this was not seen as too serious, particularly as the slow learners gained from the mixed-ability grouping.

The study, *The Quality of Pupil Learning Experiences* (Bennett *et al.*, 1984), is unusual in presenting the views of children as well as teachers on the learning in progress in the infant classrooms. These youngsters had already learned what teachers seemed to want. They had defined the situation to ease their way through potential trouble. To them the teacher's wish for 'lots of good writing' meant that the task was really about quantity, output. As long as they made the effort they would be rewarded. Procedure was given priority over understanding. Teachers were aware of the difficulty and the danger, but were mainly concerned with maintaining the level of production. Endeavour was rewarded. Meanwhile the children worked with cheerfulness and industry, concealing any cognitive problems that emerged.

To Bennett and his colleagues there were two major problems in improving the quality of work in the classroom. First, there was mis-diagnosis of the abilities and attainments of the children for the work planned. Second, there were failures in the design of the task set. This emphasis on the organisation of learning rather than on the characteristics of the children places Bennett close to Bloom (1976) in stressing the manageable features of learning, rather than those buried in the subconscious, in inheritance, or determined by social background. To raise the cognitive level of activity and to improve the management of the learning required the learning of new strategies and more thought about aims and means. Joyce and Weil's suggestion developed in Chapter 2 (pages 20–6), that teachers require a repertoire of teaching models, focuses on the same point (Joyce and Weil, 1980). To organise learning effectively means first considering what is involved in the task in hand. That is also the intention of much teacher training. The lesson plan is an attempt to match method to aim. This is a necessary procedure. It would be absurd to use the same teaching style in learning multiplication tables as for asking children to puzzle out questions about sets.

This is, of course, appreciated by the Bennett and ORACLE research teams. But researchers have to simplify the situations they investigate and generalisations about teaching styles are difficult enough without having to take account of the very different learning activities in the classrooms. The ORACLE team do, however, produce very important evidence on group work. This suggests that among primary school teachers in the 48 classrooms studied in detail group work is not only a favourite method of working but often determines the physical layout of the classroom. Grouping was recommended in the Plowden Report and seems to have been common in the early 1970s (Bealing, 1972). By the late 1970s grouping seemed universal as a way of organising the primary school classroom (Galton, Simon and Croll, 1980), but there was very little group work. Thus each child was used to being based in a group of between three and seven. They were the context in which the child worked. But that work was concentrated in individual not group tasks. The prevalence of grouping contrasted with the absence of collaborative group work. Some 90 per cent of the teachers never used such collaboration. Co-operation within the group was rare. The children sat in a group but worked as individuals.

This anomaly was further investigated by Tann (1981) as part of the ORACLE research. This was a small-scale study to see how children interacted when in a group. Twenty-four groups with four to five eleven-year-olds in each were given factual and imaginative tasks and were observed as the children worked at them. The findings confirmed the earlier evidence that there was little task-orientated interaction. The children talked to each other but still tended to work as individuals. Depressingly, it also confirmed that boys and girls at this age did not like working together.

The organisation of children into groups with work carried out individually is a major finding of the ORACLE project. It confirms that teachers have accepted the recommendations of the Plowden Committee that children should be given responsibility for their own learning. The counterpart of that is the small amount of class teaching. Indeed, when classes were large, the response was not to increase class teaching, but to try to cut down on housekeeping tasks to keep up the contacts with individual children, however slight these inevitably turned out to be. Above all, teachers having used grouping as the main means of organising the class rarely interacted with the groups formed. Only 7.5 per cent of all teacher–pupil interactions were with a group and from the pupil's point of view only 1.5 per cent. This suggests that there was no priority given to organising the children and the teaching input to maximise the collective conditions for successful learning. Even the much used project seems to have been an individual rather than a group activity. [5]

The ORACLE team suggest that primary school teachers make heavy use of project work (Leith, 1981). Curiously, with this priority, there was very little evaluation of the work done and even teachers who joined an experiment to develop instruments for evaluating projects failed to use them. The ORACLE team suggest that projects are used without much thought, possibly as a suitable means of keeping children occupied, rather than as an effective way to achieve selected ends. Once again, there does not seem to be much planning to ensure that means are matched to ends.

The final and most disturbing evidence from the ORACLE project is the reiteration of the low cognitive level of much interaction between teachers and pupils. The teachers seemed more concerned with keeping the children working than with the promotion of intellectually stimulating activity. 'Monitoring and maintaining task activity' was the concern of three-quarters of the total teacher–pupil interactions, the rest being concerned with routines. In the task-orientated interaction, only 9 per cent was observed to have a higher level cognitive content. But most of this came during interactions with the whole class and the lowest proportion in interaction with individuals. Thus individualisation does not seem to have been accompanied by any emphasis on conceptual, open-ended, challenging incursions into interaction by the teachers. When this happened it was usually in the whole class teaching. This is not to deny the value of individual or group work which can promote self-responsible learning. But once again it is difficult to see any planned relation between the method of organising the class into groups, the learning through individual work and the teacher input through talking to individual children aimed at stretching, guiding or challenging them. With some justice Thompson, one of the authors of *Breakthrough to Literacy*, reviewing the ORACLE evidence, described the demands made on the children as 'pedestrian' and the work 'dull and philistine' (Thompson, 1980).[6] Furthermore, this point about the low level of cognitive activity is also made in King (1978), Wragg (1984) and Bennett *et al.* (1984).

In these accounts of events in primary school classrooms, we are a long way from the model recommended both in the Plowden Report and in most recent psychological evidence of the conditions for effective learning. The gap between the Piaget-based recommendations in the Plowden Report and practices in the ORACLE classrooms is a feature of the evidence presented by Galton, Simon and Croll (1980). They conclude that the swing to individualisation recommended by the Committee may have been misconceived. Class sizes remained too large for sufficient attention to be given by the teacher to 20 or 30 children. In stating that there was still too much class teaching, the Plowden Committee not only underestimated the difficulties in giving each child the preparation, ongoing feedback and reinforcement that is the key to successful learning, but underestimated the potential of class teaching for probing, questioning, challenging and stretching children.

The influence of the Plowden Report can be seen in the age structure of teachers adopting different styles. Two-thirds of the individual monitors were under 30, while 90 per cent of the class enquirers were over thirty. The style changers also tended to be young. This reflected the philosophy of primary teacher training in the late 1960s and early 1970s. This may have been preparing young teachers for an impossible task, for with class sizes over 20, individualised learning was probably beyond the capacity of most teachers to cope. Certainly when this was combined with groups which were rotated during the day, or were habitually changed in an unplanned way, the attainments of the children in the ORACLE project were low compared with those in class enquirer or infrequent changer groups.[7]

The Conditions for Effective Learning

In Chapter 2, five factors were identified as being important for learning among the many psychological models and which were within the control of teachers. These were the way learning could be organised for effectiveness, the importance of advanced organisation, of ongoing feedback and reinforcement, of practice and application, and of learning as negotiation. The evidence presented in this chapter was not collected to examine the way teachers organise learning in the classroom, but does give a picture of the way children are organised, attain the basic skills and respond to different teaching styles.

The scope for structuring learning is the most obvious factor, yet is the most difficult to illuminate from evidence on the classroom. The questionnaire and the observational studies have been aimed at uncovering the consistent features of teacher behaviour, of interaction between teacher and pupils, and of the attainment of the latter. The identification and definition of consistent teaching styles seems to miss the most important point about the organisation of learning, the relation of the means employed to achieve the aims. To press this to the absurd, a class enquirer who did nothing but talk to and question the whole class, or the individual monitor who cut out even the few questions asked of pupils and just set and marked work, might be very effective on a few tasks, but would be likely to be grossly ineffective in many others. Indeed, a group instructor who only organised the work and then left the group to it would be negligent, going on the ORACLE evidence, as the major part of the work set would still be done individually.

This difficulty in detecting how teachers plan work that is appropriate for the task in hand may be due to the focus of the research projects. But even where the aim was clear, as in *Extending Beginning Reading*, the methods used seemed to be inflexible, concentrating on hearing individuals read regardless of the impossibility of giving all children this one-to-one contact for long enough to produce the intended improvement. Thus there has to be a suspicion that teachers do not give much attention to the optimum organisation of learning. For that a catholic approach would be expected in which varieties of class enquiry, group instruction, individual monitoring and style changing would be adopted as means for achieving particular ends. Thus class teaching is an efficient means of getting across factual data or getting all the children to think in a particular direction, or to feel the effect of a spoken poem. Individual work might be most effective for giving children the opportunity to push ahead in their own pursuit of knowledge, while collaborative group work, rare in the ORACLE classrooms, would be suited to developing communication skills.

The provision of advanced organisers, or cues that will alert and prepare children for the work to come, would have been included in the high level questions in the ORACLE classrooms, yet these were so rare that this kind of motivating challenge appears to have been lacking. Similarly, the ORACLE authors, looking back on their work, report that there was very little feedback or reinforcement given to the children largely because of the lack of time (Galton and Willcocks, 1983). Individual organisation seemed to have so occupied the teachers that it exhausted them trying to give all children some attention. The basic elements in successful learning seem to have been overlooked. Indeed, the descriptions of workcards as a way of keeping children busy, is one of the most depressing aspects of the research. In the one area where evaluation was deliberately promoted, project work, the teachers universally failed to use the instruments they had helped to design (Leith, 1981).

The picture drawn of the typical classroom in the ORACLE project is of busy children and an active teacher doing repetitive work. The children are described as working at time-filling tasks with 'quiet resignation'. The teachers were mostly engaged in low level, routine interactions and where quoted seemed resigned to this because of the demands made on them by some 30 children. Yet the organisation used seemed to exacerbate this problem and could account for the dependence on worksheets, projects and routine exercises to keep the children busy.

NOTES

1   The problem with such categories is that there will be variety within each cluster. It is not known whether the informal teachers were all clustered at the 'mixed' end or at the extreme of informality. Without this information it is difficult to interpret the degree of formality or informality in each category. A re-analysis of the data from the Bennett study has suggested that a different method of analysis produced very different results when teaching styles were related to pupil performance and throws doubt on the categories themselves (Aitkin, Bennett and Hesketh, 1981).

2   Categorising children is even more difficult than categorising teachers. Children are developing. Their motivation and attainments change. They are very resilient. The evidence from projects such as ORACLE should not be used to categorise individual children or the label may stick and be inappropriate, and even damaging, over time.

3   Plowden Committee was very influenced by the views of Jean Piaget, the outstanding developmental psychologist of the century. They interpreted his work as confirming that learning was an unfolding that could not be forced, and was more important than teaching. Children had to be 'ready' for learning, had to have reached the developmental stage at which skills or concepts could be mastered. Recent evidence suggests that Piaget's experiments were designed in ways that produced the results (Donaldson, 1978). Other designs have produced different evidence and shown wide variations in rates of development and the capacity of even young children for abstract thought. This implies that learning can indeed be accelerated instead of waiting for children to be 'ready' (Brown and Desforges, 1979). This new evidence has brought psychologists and educationists into line with parents and teachers who had never given up the idea that learning could be accelerated.

4   All researchers are alert to the probability of finding gaps between intention and actual practice. This makes research exciting as it gives a flavour of exposé. But teachers being investigated are on a hiding-to-nothing. Whatever they intend doing is likely to be shown to be distorted in practice. Children are very skilled at misinterpreting the intentions of teachers to the delight of social scientists.

5 Once again, this is not surprising. The surprise was that there was such an emphasis on working in, and as, a group in the Plowden Report. Children aren't fooled by teachers saying that they should work as a group and that their work will be evaluated as a group effort. They know that it is their own individual performance that is of continuous interest.

6 *Breakthrough to Literacy* was the product of an influential and widely used Schools Council Project, the Initial Literacy Project. It consists of materials related to the environment of the children and to their interests. It integrated writing, reading and speaking (Mackay, Thompson and Schaub, 1970).

7 Again, this is not surprising. If work assignments are changed in an unplanned way by 'habitual changers', the category is likely to contain a number of inefficient teachers incapable or too idle to plan work and carry it through with energy. It may be less of a category of teaching style than a judgement on the professional competence of a minority.

6 Managing Learning in the Classroom

Four sources have been used so far to establish a basis for improving the effectiveness with which learning is organised in classrooms. First, the evidence from research in the human sciences was shown to be affected by the assumptions behind the methods used. Second, similar assumptions were shown to lie behind psychological learning theories where some researchers assumed a passively responding person, while others saw active learners interpreting and adapting any stimulus. Third, sociologists were shown to model learning in schools as the product of the negotiation of meanings between teachers and learners, reflecting social differences outside the schools. Fourth, observational studies of classrooms were shown to have uncovered extensive differences between the intentions of teachers and the activity in their classrooms.

The Limitations of the Evidence

There was a double warning in the use of evidence from the human sciences as a guide to practice. A glance across a hundred years of psychology or sociology shows changes in the evidence presented as valid that made yesterday's dogma today's farce. One certainty from such a review is that tomorrow's evidence cannot be predicted except that it is sure to emphasise the bias in our contemporary views, and our unawareness of it. More optimistically, the direction of research has been away from modelling human beings as automata, to seeing them in social settings, interacting with others and thinking through situations to respond in original and often exciting ways. The shift from behaviourism to cognitive science revealed thinking, exploration, unpredictable human learning and response. Similarly sociology has shifted its focus to probe interpretations by individuals in a social setting, rather than their constraint within a social structure.

The Contribution of Psychological Learning Theories

Six personal priorities were extracted from theories of learning at the end of Chapter 2. Learning, whether simple or complex, formal or informal, starting from an appreciation of wholes or seen as built up from separate parts, requires organisation when applied to children in a classroom. There is always a need to provide cues and clues to motivate learners and alert them to the salience of factors to be presented. All learning needs to be reinforced by rewarding success and inhibiting failure. Learning requires practice and participation because it is achieved through individual activity not through the passive reception of teaching. Learning in school, as elsewhere, occurs through the individual mind, but after social interaction in which humans are engaged in the interpretation of events. Finally, it is not only humane, but productive to allow for spontaneity in learning.

The Sociological Perspective

Psychologists concerned with the influence of social interaction on learning focus on assumed human needs for approval, friendship, prestige, often through hypothesising about self-image. The sociological contribution has been to show, first, that the interaction among learners, and between them and teachers and other agents outside the school, is structured, and, second, that individuals give meanings to schooling that produce very different constructions of reality. Learning is now seen as the product of contrasting interpretations coming together in class-rooms as elsewhere. The basic sociological categories of age, sex, social class and ethnicity are used because they contain identifiable, shared interpretations which contrast with those of other groups. Furthermore, the language in which learning is negotiated is itself not only a distinguishing characteristic of the groups involved, but is closely related to the underlying political, economic and social relations which determine prospects in school and work.

The Observations of Classroom Practices

Once learning was looked at in the context of one teacher and many children in a classroom, the restraints, disturbances and logistical problems became the foreground of learning. The observations showed gaps between the intentions of teachers and the way these worked out in practice. This applied to the organisation of work where many children wasted much of their time, and to the low level of much of the activity in which children were engaged.

The rest of this chapter unashamedly involves 'tips for teachers'. No excuse is needed for mining the available evidence to produce an *aide-memoire* to help in the planning of learning in the classroom. If the investment in the human sciences directed at human learning cannot help where it matters, a lot of resources and effort are being squandered. However, there have been many attempts to mine the reliable and valid, and the overlap between them is not only predictable, but comforting. Most have selected similar factors as important and organised them in overlapping schemes for planning learning. This suggests not only that research has produced a body of evidence that is a dependable basis for recommending action, but that this is relevant to teachers amid the bustle of classrooms.[1]

Here are two schemes devised by psychologists reviewing the evidence available from psychology and from studies of learning in the classroom. Bloom (1976) concentrates on individual differences in learning which can be predicted, explained and altered, while rejecting individual differences in learners as a profitable focus because they deflect attention from factors in the classroom that are under the control of teachers. This optimism of Bloom at the end of a distinguished career which started with a fatalistic view of the early determination of differences between children (Bloom, 1964) is re-visited in Chapter 7. Here the important feature is the emphasis on improving school learning. Similarly Stones (1979), by examining the similarities between teachers and psychologists as they look for ways of improving learning, concentrates on factors that can be managed rather than on those that seem pre-destined, innate or fixed at an early age.

B. S. Bloom*

Bloom sees the history of the learner at the core of school learning. Each one enters a new learning situation with a different history. This contrasts with the conventional psychological approach to experimentation on learning where previous history is controlled out of consideration. The model presented by Bloom emphasises the factors that follow.

1. *Student characteristics*
   Cognitive entry behaviours – a history of previous learning.
   Affective entry characteristics – a history leading to distinctive motivation towards the task in hand.
2. *Instruction*
   Learning tasks presented, explained and ordered to be optimum for each learner. In particular, the provision of:
   cues;
   participation;
   reinforcement;
   feedback/correctives.

E. Stones†

Stones uses the term psychopedagogy to mean the application of theoretical principles from psychology to the practice of teaching. Like Bloom his interest is in teaching, rather than teachers. The model presented by Stones follows this sequence:

1. *Pre-active*
   Analysis of task to be tackled.
   Checking the necessary prerequisite competences of pupils.
2. *Interactive*
   Cueing the pupils for the task.
   Encouraging exploration, activity and analysis of the task.

---

* *Human Characteristics and School Learning* (1976) Maidenhead: McGraw-Hill.
† *Psychopedagogy* (1979) and *Supervision in Teacher Education* (1984). London: Methuen.

   Reminding pupils of the important features of the task and
      providing prompts and possible methods of solution.
   Providing feedback.
3   *Evaluation*
   Promoting generalisation of learning to new problems.

The overlap between these two models results from their
common concern with improving teaching and learning rather
than with the styles of teachers or learners. Both contain the
same emphasis on the knowledge, skills and attitudes that
children bring to the task set, on the nature of that task, and on
the importance of establishing motivation, and sustaining it
throughout the task by the provision of reinforcement to
encourage successful performance, and feedback to the learner
to give information on the effects of the actions taken.
Furthermore, both use a three stage model consisting of a
consideration of competences available at entry to the task, of an
analysis of the task itself and of sustained motivation and
guidance as it proceeds, ends and is evaluated.

Obviously the summaries of the models above are gross over-
simplifications. But the objective is to extract the common
elements for later use. Hence the next step is to take into account
the three aspects of learning covered in Chapters 2 to 5. From
psychology the two contrasting models from Gagné (1965) and
Ausubel (1968) are summarised. The focus then shifts to the
gaps between intention and practice once classrooms are observed, before adding sociological evidence.

Top-down and Bottom-up Models for Teaching

Learning can be conceived as starting with parts to be built into a
whole, or as an initial consideration of the whole. One is
incremental and bottom-up, the other reflective and top-down.
Neither is necessarily superior, for the task may determine the
optimum organisation for learning. Clearly it would be absurd to
ask children to reflect on multiplication tables without giving
them the bottom-up, incremental exercises that will bring them
quickly to the point where reflection would be rewarding. On the
other hand there are many areas of human experience that would
be destroyed by an incremental approach. This not only applies
to feelings about Spring, but to much problem-solving in basic
skills.

R. N. Gagné

Gagné's (1965) approach is bottom-up. The first step in effective teaching is to analyse the task in hand, breaking it down into parts that can be placed in sequence from simple to complex. The children are then led through the stages, with the teacher helping them to make the connection from one stage to the next more complicated one. Ausubel (1963) takes the opposite, top-down, approach, starting at the conceptual level. The objective is to make learning meaningful rather than concentrating on analysis of the task. Advanced organisers are the means of introducing learners to the concepts which will enable the facts and ideas that follow to be organised and understood. Gagné and Ausubel share an emphasis on starting with what the children already know. But Gagné breaks up the task as a start to building a model for teachers and lays less emphasis on the processes of learning than on the organisation of the subject matter. Obviously some tasks are suitable for this sequencing from simple to complex, but others depend on imaginative jumps that are not the concern of this incremental, linear model. Mathematics may often be linear, but English is rarely so sequenced. Ausubel, on the other hand, by starting at the conceptual level, may be presenting a model that is unsuitable for many of the tasks facing young children. Here a more concrete approach may often be needed. Once again, no single model is likely to suffice. Different tasks and different children may require different approaches. [2]

Gagné starts with a selection of mental activities seen as central to any learning. He then ranks them into a sequence wherein one has to be mastered before the next can be tackled. The task of the teachers is to organise the conditions under which the learners have the best chance of working through the sequence to the most advanced problem-solving, the ability to apply all the previous learning. The strength of this model is in stressing the individual nature of learning, but also the part played by teachers in facilitating this by thinking through the stages in learning. Thus there is a model, a strategy for organising learning that accompanies the hierarchy of mental activities involved. It is this twin concern with the sequences in learning and the ways the passage through them can be facilitated by the teacher that makes Gagné's model so useful.

The six key activities in the learning hierarchy are as follows:

Specific responding is a simple stimulus-response sequence. The teacher presents the stimulus of a picture of a cat and the children sing out 'cat'. Much learning through reading, looking, listening is of this simple response kind.

Chaining is the linking of responses into series. Most activities or knowledge about the world consists of such sequences of responses strung together by the learner.

Multiple discrimination is the process of sorting out responses and chains of responses to apply in very different contexts. Children may have mastered the four rules for handling numbers, but still have to learn to apply them in practice.

Classifying consists of grouping objects and ideas according to some understood principle. This is concept learning, appreciating what is common among animals, or verbs, or how food and growth are related for living things.

Rule-using enables concepts to be applied in general form. Thus children learn 'i before e, except after c' and apply it as new 'ie' or 'ei' words are met. The rules move learning from the particular to the general.

Problem-solving involves the application of several rules to new situations and issues.

To Gagné each of these increasingly complicated forms of learning rests on mastering lower forms. Thus chaining can only come after specific responses have been mastered. Problem-solving depends on the prior learning of rule-using which in turn rests on classifying and so on. There are several attempts at producing such a hierarchy of learning (see, for example, Bloom, 1956). They point to the important task of the teacher in ensuring that the conditions for increasingly complex learning are established. There is however some objection to this linear view of learning. It ignores leaps to complicated thinking, insights that do not seem to depend on previously learned skills.

Gagné has provided a list of tasks that can help teachers to lead learners through his hierarchy of learning. Once again this is a useful *aide-memoire*, a practical reminder for teachers of steps that can ease the way to learning.

Informing the learner of the objectives of the exercise – to prepare and motivate the learner by advanced organisers.

Presenting stimuli – by means of visual aids or introductions or stories that increase interest.

Increasing the learner's attention – by questions on the stimuli presented.

Helping recall – by reminding the children of related work or experiences.

Providing conditions that lead to performance – by setting exercises to make the children to think for themselves.

Determining sequences of learning – to lead children through the hierarchy of learning towards rule-using and problem-solving.

Prompting and guiding learning – to put the children in a position to learn for themselves.

The practical nature of these learning and instructional models brings them close to the pragmatic advice given to student teachers on the planning of learning. This often goes as follows: 'simple to complex, practical to theoretical, interest and motivate, give advanced information on intended outcomes, sequence the work, plan for different speeds of mastery and don't stop at learning, move to generalisation and practice'. All the practical hints can be found in the learning models. Hints and models contain many contradictions, but the message is usually that learning needs organising, whether it is intended to come from the children through their own imagination or experience or through teachers building up the individual child's knowledge and self-discipline. Once again it is not coincidence that Herbart's *Science of Education*, first published in 1806, has strikingly similar recommendations for teachers to Gagné's *Conditions of Learning* (1965).[3] Each places the responsibility for children learning firmly with the teacher. Learning for Gagné is an individual matter. But the conditions for it have to be organised and the sequence of planning for teachers has not changed much in over 150 years.

D. P. Ausubel

Ausubel (1968) starts by distinguishing between meaningful and rote learning. The former rests on conceptual learning, while the latter lacks the potential for extending, transforming and applying the knowledge acquired, because it lacks the conceptual base from which these can spring. This is a common distinction, but Ausubel goes further in stressing how meaningful, concept-based learning can be organised and taught. He does not see it as only the product of individual problem-solving.

The key is to prepare the learner and organise the task so that meaningful learning can occur. This is the purpose served by the advanced organiser, getting the learner set by the introduction of conceptual material that will prepare for the work to come. The art teacher explains how the availability of materials tends to determine the style of building in different places at different periods, and gets the children to think about this before setting them to work studying pre-industrial, early industrial and recent, reinforced concrete constructions. The mathematics teacher discusses the way we group similar things before moving to the study of sets.

To Ausubel, the advanced organiser is a way of securing an active learner. This can occur as much when the teacher is expounding as when the children are organised to search out information for themselves. The central feature of successful learning is activity by the learner, regardless of the teacher- or child-centred nature of the organisation employed. The task of organising learning starts with the structure of subjects, identifying the key concepts and then teaching them to children. These views on the way subjects can be analysed conceptually and then taught in schools so that the structure of the subject disciplines rather than details of content are mastered, lie behind many recent curriculum projects, particularly in science and mathematics. The limited success of these developments and the tendency for more stress to be put on the basic skills and facts in the 1970s, suggests that it has limitations as an approach to teaching. This stress on the structure of subjects contained one recurring truth. Over-dependence on the memorising of facts was stultifying. The emphasis on meaningful learning did introduce more scientific or historical or creative study into the school curriculum and helped teachers to organise learning aimed at understanding and application, imagination and exploration.

The lasting influence of these approaches stressing conceptual learning can be seen in curriculum planning through notions such as key ideas, and in teaching as highly structured but aimed at meaningful learning. The emphasis on concepts has softened, but the identification of the key ideas in a subject such as geography remains. Many modern textbooks are organised on this principle and authors usually identify the crucial knowledge, ideas and attitudes. This is the way the Assessment of Performance Unit working groups set about defining language, mathematics, science, aesthetics, physical development and social and personal development as cross-curricular topics,[4] and is the way teachers now tend to think through their longer-term aims within subject areas. It is difficult to appreciate that this has been a development that accelerated only in the 1960s. The curriculum development movement may have had a limited impact, but it spread a more imaginative, deeper and structural view of subject teaching.

The effect on teaching of the view that subjects not only have distinctive structures but that these can be taught, has been equally influential. To Ausubel, there is a parallel between the way subjects are organised and the way knowledge is organised in the human mind. It is a simple and rather obvious, but often neglected, point. Subjects are human constructions. Over time they come to be seen as objective, 'out there'. But they are also part of the way we come to perceive the world. As we learn history we come to see our world historically. A sociologist 'sees' things in a different way from a psychologist because each uses a different set of concepts to organise their views. Teaching the structure of subjects is a key part of helping individuals to see the world in ways determined by centuries of accumulated knowledge within changing, but at any one time distinct, subjects. To Ausubel, this requires highly organised directive teaching. General ideas are presented first. These are then broken down into details and built up into new ideas. Both differentiation and integration are the responsibility of teachers.

Gagné's list of tasks to help teachers guide children towards the point where they can learn for themselves contains the cueing, stimulating, motivating, prompting, practising and sequencing that recur in such *aides-memoire* based in psychology. To Ausubel, it is the emphasis rather than the content which is different, for the effort is directed towards putting the learner in a position where effort can be self-sustained. But another look at the lists provided by Bloom, Stones or Gagné will show that learning is modelled as something organised for children rather than interpreted by them. Even when the task is to master an obviously useful skill such as reading or swimming, the motivation to learn and the meaning given to the learning might be crucial in determining success. Bloom comes nearest to this in emphasising effective entry characteristics. But these are seen as motivational or to do with self-image rather than tied to the social, ethnic or sexual backgrounds of the child.

It may seem far-fetched to suggest that the organisation of learning in the classroom needs to take account of race, sex and class, yet each has been shown to be the basis of different achievement. Furthermore, the issues are now part of educational policy. The Inner London Education Authority, for example, has published priorities for action to eradicate unjust policies (ILEA, 1983). These include sections on the curriculum, styles and methods of teaching, and staff relationships with pupils. This adds another dimension to models for guiding the organisation of learning, linking them to the social and political structure outside the school and to the way teachers and learners interact within it.

The concern with groups who do not share the culture of most teachers has been focused on the role of language in education. From a concern to remedy deficiencies in languages used by minorities, the emphasis has switched to stressing their value. Mother-tongue teaching is a legal obligation throughout the European Community. Planning the organisation of learning has to take account of language both as communication and as something valued in its own right.

The Gap between Intention and Practice

When the evidence from Chapters 4 and 5 is taken into account, the spotlight for effective planning switches to the gap between the intentions of teachers and their realisation in the classroom. While caution is necessary because this gap between ideal and real, intended and actual, is usually revealed when researchers observe, or collect, the accounts of the different parties involved, this evidence produces a new set of priorities. Looking across Bennett et al., 1980; Bennett et al., 1984; Galton et al., 1980a, 1980b and 1983; Southgate et al., 1981 and Wragg, 1984, a series of weaknesses in the organisation of learning becomes apparent in the assessment of the abilities of children, the tasks they are set, and the way these are organised in classrooms.

The most disturbing common finding in recent classroom studies has been the low level of most of the work. This has been most dramatically illustrated by Kerry (1984). In the mixed ability classrooms studied only four per cent of verbal transactions and 15 per cent of tasks were classified as 'stimulating' for the pupils. Over half the teacher–pupil interactions were routine management. Even where transactions were concerned with work-in-hand, they were mainly an exchange of information, not involving ideas or intellectual challenge.

This low level of most activity in the classrooms observed overlapped with the undifferentiated nature of work in the mixed ability classes under observation. The low level was necessary because work had not been organised to cater for individual differences through the use of individualised or collaborative group work. The work was aimed at the middle range of ability. The most and least able were often left bored or stranded. In Bennett et al. (1984), over half the tasks set were classified as too easy or too difficult. In particular high attaining children were underestimated in setting number and language tasks. Like the low attainers who were often confused, they kept working with apparent cheerfulness, but they were suffering from problems in the assessment of their ability in relation to the task set.

The setting of tasks is particularly difficult in mixed ability classrooms. But even when the task is suitable it may be worked at by children in unintended ways. In the Bennett et al., 1984 study, 30 per cent of number and 20 per cent of language tasks were implemented in ways not intended by the teachers. This was particularly the case with 'incremental' as distinct from 'practice' tasks. Furthermore, the children were able to keep working through changing the nature of the tasks, usually by making them routine exercises. Teachers enabled this to happen by rewarding the quantity rather than the quality of work.

The ability of teachers to keep children working by rewarding their efforts and of children to adapt tasks set to their own style and level of industry tends to conceal problems in the organisation of effective learning. Added to the difficulties in assessing and coping with the varied entry characteristics of the children, these task construction problems complicate lesson planning. But there is a third difficulty for teachers. All the observational studies show the logistical problems in coping with many children often working as individuals. Most of the classrooms were seen as busy, cheerful places. But there were wide variations in the working habits of children and a lot of time wasted in waiting for the teacher's attention either in a queue or with a hand up or by the occasional plea of 'Please'.

Thus the classroom observations supplement the models for teaching at the planning and implementation stages. The importance of careful diagnosis of the abilities and attainments of pupils as they are prepared for the task is underlined. So is the planning of the work and its relation to these pupil characteristics. Finally, this evidence grounds the management of learning in the classroom bustle. The neat sequences recommended may be based on reliable academic evidence, but teachers have to manage a flow of crises and these can disturb the best of learning strategies.

The Key Factors in the Management of Learning

Out of all the many attempts to ground the organisation of learning in the classroom in the evidence it is possible to select the commonly accepted key factors. The result is not dramatic nor very different from the common sense planning used by all teachers, for they are concerned with the same aspects and procedures as psychologists or other experts. The difference is in the systematic approach of the latter and the pressure on the former to take the reality of the classroom into consideration.

Such an attempt to move to prescription incorporates several assumptions and raises several objections. It assumes that all learning, whether teacher-directed or open-ended, is enhanced by the creation of an appropriate environment. Second, it assumes that the job of the teacher is to organise and manage that environment. Third, it assumes that it is possible for teachers to know, and plan in relation to, the knowledge, skills and attitudes of children in the class. All of these assumptions are open to challenge. Any organisation of learning can be seen as a denial of the natural capacity of children to seek and find worthwhile knowledge and values. Management can be seen as exploitation, a distortion of individual development. Matching the learning environment to the capacities of children can be seen as discrimination and hence exploitation. However, the observational evidence suggests that most teachers accept a responsibility to organise the context if not the content of learning. It has also been argued that the organisation is more, not less, necessary when the purpose is to encourage spontaneity. It is certainly more difficult to arrange.

Three aspects emerge from the models so far presented. There is the consideration of the entry characteristics of the pupils in relation to the activity planned. Secondly, there is the task itself. Thirdly, there is the organisation of activities to enable that task to be mastered or for the children to use it creatively. This gives a basic model for planning.

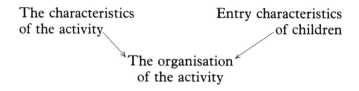

The characteristics   Entry characteristics
of the activity   of children
                The organisation
                of the activity

Here another assumption should be noted. There is no emphasis on either innate or environmental factors that determine learning. It is assumed that teachers can plan effectively to raise attainment.

The characteristics of the activity

Task analysis through which intended learning is defined in sufficient detail to serve as a basis for planning can range from a casual consideration by a teacher just before a lesson, to a detailed specification of learning objectives. The steps that follow are a guide to ensure that the learning intended has been thought through in sufficient detail.

1 *Defining what is to be learned*
    What are the learners expected to learn, practise or experience?
    Is the learning concerned with knowledge, skills, attitudes or some combination of these?
    Is the intention to introduce new ideas, skills or values or to lead children towards discovering these?
    Is the intention to practise or revise?
2 *Deciding on the resources required*
    Does the task require special facilities inside or outside the classroom?
    Does the task require any special arrangement of the classroom?
    Does the task require written or audio or visual resources?
    How is the teacher going to act as a resource?

3   *Deciding what is a measure of successful learning*
What would be accepted as evidence that the intended learning had been achieved?
Is it possible to spell out criteria of acceptable performance?

The characteristics of the children at entry to the task

Once again, consideration of entry characteristics can range from a rapid review of the previous learning related to the task and of the enthusiasm for this area of work, to a survey of the social background, tests of attainment and ability, and an analysis of the content in relation to the values held by the children. The basic questions are as follows:

1   *Establishing the connection to earlier work*
While much learning is not sequential or linear, it is safest to ask:
Have all children the necessary prior knowledge to benefit from the new task?
What steps will be necessary to establish a sufficient basis for learning?
Do the entry characteristics in relation to the tasks point to individual, group or whole class work?
2   *Matching the work to the children*
Ideally work should stretch children but not be beyond them. These questions check out the matching of task to attainment and ability.
Is the work likely to engage fully the bright children?
Is it likely to be beyond the less able child?
Is the intention that children should do the work at the same speed or at their own individual rates or at rates within groups?
How is the work to be organised to allow for different rates of progress?
3   *Allowing for motivation*
Children tend to approach work with different degrees of enthusiasm. They may be emotionally disturbed by it or see it in ways that not only differ from those of other children, but from the teacher. This can be checked by asking the following:
Is there anything about this work that will be offensive to any of the children?

Are there any material, physiological or social factors that may interfere with successful learning?

Is the learning organised so that all children will experience personal achievement?

Is the introduction to the work sufficiently motivating?

The organisation of the activity

The view taken in this book has been that activity is not an end in itself. 'Busyness' is not necessarily rewarding. Hence the organisation of activity is to achieve some aim specified by the teacher, although that might be to initiate action by children which has no pre-specified outcome. But whether the aim is to promote new learning directly, or to promote the skills that will enable the children to explore ideas and practices themselves, the means employed will be directed at previously specified aims.

1 *Preparing the children for the task*
The evidence in Chapters 4 and 5 of this book suggested that children were not only kept busy in most cases, but persisted cheerfully even when understanding little of the intentions of the teacher in setting the work. The most prevalent example was converting exercises designed to get the children to think, explore and extend their thinking, into routine practice of already mastered skills. Thus it is useful to ask the following questions in planning:

Do the children know the purpose of the activity?

Do they know what they are supposed to be doing?

Is the work organised to avoid purposeless activity taking over?

2 *Keeping the work rewarding*
Is the work organised to provide feedback to the children on how well they are doing, without excessive dependence on the teacher?

Is there sufficient reinforcement of successful learning through speedy rewards, and sufficient inhibiting of unsuccessful responses to stop these being learned?

Is the work graduated to lead children towards more advanced skills such as problem-solving?

Are there opportunities built in for children to think for themselves, express their thoughts and have them valued?

3 *Controlling the quality of work*

One of the most remarkable aspects of the classroom observation studies reported in Chapters 4 and 5 was the variations in the time spent working by different children and within different classrooms. When that is added to the many examples of gaps between the teacher's intentions and the work actually done by the children, it is clear that teachers also require regular feedback to evaluate their efforts. But that is related to the role that the teacher is to play as a manager of resources for learning, or as a resource himself or herself. The recurring evidence of time-wasting due to the common insistence on trying to deal with up to 30 children individually, suggests that teachers are not cost-effective in the allocation of their own time and energy. Hence the following questions need to be asked:

> How is the teacher's time to be allocated between being a resource for children and managing their learning?
>
> Given the logistics of classrooms, what is the optimum use of the teacher's time, given the activity planned?
>
> Is it possible to minimise management tasks in order to free time for helping children to higher level activities?
>
> Can criteria of success be established for the activity?
>
> What evaluation can be built into the planning of the activity to provide information based on pre-specified criteria, or, where this is not possible, on indicators referred to during and after the activity?

This crude *aide-memoire* is probably close to the questions asked implicitly by all teachers as they plan their work. It has the advantage of using insights from the evidence spelled out in earlier chapters. But it is crude and would provide only a basis for a more useful, personal guide for individual teachers. Once subject interest, content and approaches are taken into account, a new range of questions become important. The environment of the school, its internal organisation, the philosophy of the teacher, the age of the children, their backgrounds and the support they receive from parents, all add further questions. It remains an example, not an exemplar.

NOTES

1   It is important to re-emphasise the inevitable bias in the selection of these 'tips for teachers'. As a white, anglo-saxon, agnostic, middle-class sociologist with a large mortgage, I have, no doubt, views that differ from those held by others differently blessed.

2   This places responsibility on teachers to be discriminating and critical when being advised on methods of teaching or when reading books on learning. Teaching and learning can be analysed as if free of particular contexts, but in schools they are context-bound. Furthermore, that context in schools consists of a variety of learning tasks, heterogeneous children and parents, and teacher-pupil and pupil-pupil relations that are often unpredictable and are always in a state of flux.

3   J. F. Herbart was Immanuel Kant's successor as Professor of Philosophy at the University of Konigsburg and an influential writer on pedagogy, the science of teaching. His views remained influential in teacher training into the twentieth century and can still be found in the more formal plans for lessons asked for in the preparation for teaching practice.

4   The Assessment of Performance Unit (APU) was established by the Department of Education and Science in 1974. Emphasis at the start was on the diagnosis of the difficulties experienced by disadvantaged children. Later, the emphasis changed to the monitoring of standards of attainment over time. More recently, the results of testing have been used to promote discussion about the curriculum of mathematics, science and language.

7 Promoting Learning, Avoiding Determinism

This review of evidence on the organisation of learning has produced two sets of complementary information, one describing what seems to be going on in contemporary primary school classrooms, the other suggesting steps that could be used to improve the effectiveness of teaching. While it is not easy to extract the dependable evidence as a basis for recommendation, it is clear that learning is often organised either with little concern for effectiveness, or with little attention to the key factors identified in the human sciences.

There are two assumptions underlying this concluding chapter that have recurred throughout the book. First, that it is possible to promote learning, whether seen as subject- or child-centred. All learning is ultimately achieved by individuals. Whether the emphasis is on teaching or on providing a context in which children learn for themselves, their organisation within a prepared context is essential. It is even more difficult to organise for children to find out for themselves. Later in this chapter the weakness in the long-term planning of learning as systematic enquiry recommended by Piaget will be discussed. He may have given the research base for child-centred activity, but he shared with Skinner, the leading proponent of programmed instruction, a concern with the essential structure of learning. That concern is common to all learning theorists.

The second assumption of this chapter is that it is more beneficial to focus attention on the manageable, the alterable, than upon forces beyond the control of teachers. It is interesting academically to relate human behaviour to the sweep of history, the hidden depths of the mind, to genetics, to industrialisation, capitalism or the class structure. Each exerts its influence, but they are beyond control in the classroom, and belief that they are overwhelming leads to fatalism. None of the evidence is sufficiently convincing for teachers to ignore their responsibility to employ the forces under their control to improve attainment as far as possible. Furthermore, the use of explanations in terms of culture, social background, inheritance and so on, often conceals individual responsibility for events. There are social class differences in attainment, but it is the decisions of parents to choose this form of schooling, of politicians to press for these policies, of teachers to inspire or bore children, that decide the future of individual children (Shipman, 1984). The categories are useful, but they can conceal personal responsibility and be an excuse for inaction.

The Promotion of Learning

The picture of the primary school classroom drawn in Chapters 4 and 5 is of 'busyness' and of time spent by children on work set. The teacher was clearly in charge. Children were organised into groups, set to work and kept working by teachers who also fixed seating arrangements, groups and the pace and style of working.

Children were mainly organised into groups but worked as individuals (Galton and Simon, 1980). This does not mean that they were unaffected by the presence of others. There is, of course, talk and interaction within the groups. However, this is usually distracting rather than contributing to the task in hand (Bennett et al., 1984). In the Bennett et al. studies of infant schools, the one tenth of interactions that were related to the task were of a procedural or personal nature, not exchanges of ideas. This applied particularly to less able children. This is frustrating given the Plowden Committee's insistence that children '... make their meaning clearer by having to explain it to others ...' (Plowden Report (DES, 1967) paragraph 757) and group work leads to increasing understanding (paragraph 758). The most disappointing aspect of the descriptive evidence is the low level of the intellectual activity reported. This arises partly from the failure of grouping to result in collaborative learning. It also arises from the role adopted by teachers. By attempting to maximise contacts with individual children, teachers spread their influence very thin. Contacts with children are measured in seconds only (Resnick, 1972; Brandt, 1975). Each discussion tends to be brief and subject to interruption. Furthermore, attention is very unevenly distributed (Garner and Bing, 1973).

The content also tended to be about procedures or behaviour rather than the issues being studied. Teachers rarely talked to groups and the effort to deal with individuals led to time-wasting, queueing and an uneven distribution of the teachers' attention.

The descriptive evidence probably piles on the agony by starting with a norm of 100 per cent time-on-task. In practice much of the apparently haphazard chatter may be valuable experience. Working as individuals while being part of a group may be a natural situation for children. They can get on with the work but act sociably. The ORACLE project's solitary workers formed one-third of the children and put in most work, but their single-mindedness could not have all been gain. They may have been achieving tunnel vision in their perception of worthwhile learning.

What then could the evidence suggest as ways of increasing the effectiveness of learning, including the depth of intellectual activity? Six factors were identified in Chapter 2 (pages 26–32). These were:

- that learning in all its variety could be organised;
- that children needed to be prepared for the learning tasks;
- that the learning should be reinforced;
- that knowledge skills and attitudes need to be developed through practice and participation;
- that learning is negotiation as well as transmission;
- that scope should be left for children to pursue their own interests.

There are two unusual features of these factors for the organisation of effective learning. They are more concerned with the quality of teaching than the characteristics of teachers, and with the attainments of children before and after learning than with their intelligence. This brings them into line with contemporary cognitive psychology (see, for example, Bloom, 1981). It is a hopeful approach, concentrated on organising teaching and learning, rather than analysing personality or intelligence. It assumes that given a learning environment appropriately constructed for the task in hand and adequate time, all children will learn. That is the opposite of many assumptions built into contemporary schooling where children are sorted out by ability and given separate learning experiences which further widen any initial differences.

The second unusual feature is that knowledge is not assumed to be packages handed from teacher to child without question, but a spectrum of messages ranging from the absolute to the relative, the universal to the negotiable. Multiplication tables may be transmitted without question, but peace studies are clearly negotiable. However, there are not only many aspects of the curriculum that are seen to be very different from varying social, political, ethnic or sexual viewpoints, but others where it is not reasonable to assume that teachers should direct activity authoritatively. Feeling, expressing and creating, can rarely be programmed and are usually crabbed by the effort to do so. The opportunities to appreciate Spring have to be provided, but not instructions on how to do it.

There is of course nothing unusual about the list of factors behind the effective organisation for learning. But the evidence from studies of classrooms suggests that they are not applied systematically. The organisation is not always tailored to the task in hand. Children are not motivated to tackle it, nor is there the quick feedback that reinforces learning, or the practice that deepens and extends it. Indeed, the classroom organisation often seems haphazard, without any apparent matching of the tasks to the relative attainments of the children or to the salient features of the subject.

It is of course easy to point to the problems and recommend solutions. It is difficult to implement them with 30 children in a classroom. Yet the descriptive evidence suggests that teachers tend to adopt methods that minimise the chances of being able to maximise learning. Furthermore, by attempting to adopt a one-to-one base for teaching, they increase the problems of organising the remaining 29 children. The low level of intellectual activity may be partly the result of a deliberate choice of methods that have an impossible logic. There is no way one adult can deal with the continuously changing intellectual, behavioural and procedural problems of a class of children on an individual basis. The organisation of learning has to be adjusted to that situation.

Most of the American evidence on effective teaching points to the ability to maximise active learning time as crucial. Kounin (1970), Dunkin and Biddle (1974), Brophy and Evertson (1976), all point to smoothness in organisation and control as the key factors. Kounin, for example, isolates as important 'with-it-ness', 'smoothness', 'momentum', 'group alerting' (keeping an eye on those who slack), 'overlappingness' (dealing with two or more issues at the same time), and above all 'variety and challenge' in the tasks set. Of course, this is rather like recommending good health as a way of avoiding illness. But these characteristics do contain one common feature that recurs as a thread through the evidence available. Successful teaching is organised. This is also the conclusion of English research. The more consistent and sustained the management, the more involved in work were the children (Law, 1977). Similarly, Bennett (1979) focuses on the management of attention as central to effective teaching. However, this is only one factor and learning involves many. The ORACLE evidence does not show active learning time as important (Galton and Simon, 1980).

This stress on the management of learning is optimistic. It implies that teachers can arrange learning situations to ensure that children are motivated and organised to learn. It places the responsibility firmly with the teacher to plan work effectively. However obvious, that responsibility is often overlooked through assumptions that learning, being child-centred, requires minimal teacher intervention, whereas the opposite is the case as the context has to be more adequately prepared than for class teaching. The importance of organising learning is often obscured by an emphasis on the impact of factors in the social background of the children outside the school. But learning is achieved by individual children. Around the statistical averages individuals succeed and fail. The organisation of learning is a means of achieving a fairer as well as a more efficient education.

This concern with justice as well as efficiency brings the book back to the concern with research methods in Chapter 1. It is possible to conceal the tragedy for individual children behind the statistics relating to social class or ethnic group. It is also possible to conceal the responsibility of teachers behind these and other categories. The problem is dehumanised, converted into impersonal concepts. But the use of these concepts to explain situations is part of the danger in research already identified. If you conceptualise intelligence you can explain low attainment by reference to it. The same applies to the moving force of history, to genes, to the sub-conscious, maternal deprivation, social background, culture and self-concept. Each provides explanations, but each provides a reason for not expecting and striving for improvement. The explanation simultaneously provides a reason for expecting failure and condoning it.

Avoiding Determinism

If there is one message in this book about the evidence on learning in the classroom or elsewhere, it is that humans, young or old, are capable of breaking any prediction about behaviour and that teaching should acknowledge this. Optimism that human ingenuity will frustrate attempts to formulate laws that limit it, can be gauged from the numerous examples in natural and human science where inexorable laws collapsed under some breakthrough from human initiative (Shipman, 1981). When the President of the American Astronomical Society, Simon Newcomb, could still write papers on the impossibility of powered flight three years after the Wright brothers achieved it in 1903,[1] when a generation of Russian biologists could be misled by Lysenko,[2] when Cyril Burt could maintain his theories by fraud,[3] scepticism becomes a duty, and faith in human ingenuity becomes a realistic antidote to determinist theories.

In the human sciences it is a long way from constructing a model of human learning to implementing it in the classroom. The hypotheses derived, the methods of enquiry chosen, the evidence collected, its selection, interpretation and adaptation to teaching, and its adjustment to take account of differences among children, teachers and curricula, all provide scope for application and amendment beyond that intended by the originator of the theory. But the most important aspect of this sequence of translating theory into practice lies in the way both dogmatism and determinism have been built into the interpretations and recommendations. Instead of promoting ingenuity, the use of psychological and sociological evidence has often generated ideas of helplessness among learners whose behaviour was seen as determined by genes, history or contemporary environment.

Part of this determinism has arisen from attempts to model human behaviour on one or a few powerful factors, whether inherited or acquired, while ignoring not only the many other pressures, but the human capacity for making the past, the biology, the social background and early experience poor guides to the present. The second source of determinism has been the selection of factors in research and the control exercised. Learning was seen to result from factors not open to control by teachers because those that could be organised to help learning in the classroom were often ignored or controlled out of consideration. This applied in particular to the accumulated learning of children as they were given new tasks, their individual and relevant experiences at that time and the way the tasks were set. These are the factors in the forefront for the teacher, but have often been controlled out of consideration by researchers to enable the effects of simpler factors to be observed. This applies not only to experimental psychology but to surveys and observational studies. The focus has been on the predictable, on regularities, the categories of the behaviour, not the capacity of children to do the unexpected.

The third reason why human science has often given a rather hopeless, fatalistic view of learning in the classroom is that communication is usually seen as unproblematic. The problem is defined as the failure of the learner to master knowledge considered as universally valuable. But the addition of sociological evidence has shown not only the way environmental influences affect responses in the classroom, but the way that knowledge is itself constructed, negotiated and evaluated as interaction takes place between teachers and learners. The message received is not necessarily that transmitted!

The final reason why the human sciences have tended to reduce efforts to raise human attainment at the same time as producing the evidence of inequality is that they have been accorded an excessive authority. Evidence is a supplement to, not a replacement for, professional judgement. Yet it is often used as authoritative because the concepts are seductive. Terms like social class, intelligence, social background and motivation conceal the real complexity. That is the value of concepts. They enable diverse elements to be grouped together so that thinking about them can be generalised. Imagine trying to explain differential attainment without using the term social class. But the gathering together over-simplifies and conceals the individual diversity.

There is, however, an even more misleading feature of the conceptual frameworks used in the human sciences. They confuse attribution with explanation. In Chapter 2 it was stressed that learning theories do not explain how humans learn, they model it from observations of what seems to be going on as learning occurs. That is very useful, for we do not have to know how something works in order to make it more effective. It is useful to identify social class, gender, ethnic group and so on as important factors in school attainment. But they are signposts only when the concern is with particular individual cases. They should never be used to explain a learning difficulty. That is likely to lie in a complicated set of individual circumstances. Thus it is important to avoid seeing the human sciences as 'proving', or uncovering 'causes', or 'explaining', and to avoid using labels such as 'working class', as if this was a homogeneous group that does not contain individuals whose life styles frequently make such a grouping absurd. Above all, the concepts should never be a replacement for the search for factors in the previous history of the child, or the best way of planning the task in hand when learning is being organised.

Recent changes in approach within the human sciences have reduced the determinism in the evidence produced. Teachers are now more likely to meet evidence that deals with factors that are within their control, rather than innate, or fixed in infancy, or determined by the unfolding of history. As this nineteenth century determinism has been rejected, the evidence available tends to illuminate the ingenuity of human thought and action. That gives teachers a more hopeful as well as a more important role in the promotion of learning.

NOTES

1   Simon Newcomb was a Professor of mathematics as well as vice-president of the US National Academy of Sciences and director of the American Nautical Almanac Office. He was largely responsible for the ideas in H. G. Wells's *The Time Machine* through his paper on the Fourth Dimension. Unfortunately news of the Wright brothers' flight appeared in the journal *Gleanings in Bee Culture*, which is rarely read by august scientists. Curiously the event received little immediate publicity and poor Professor Newcomb went on writing of the impossibility of powered flight long after it had taken place.

2   T. D. Lysenko dominated Russian biology under Stalin. His critics were often arrested and exiled. This inhibited the adoption of Mendelian genetic theories in the USSR and led to experiments in agriculture that produced ambitious five year plans but no extra food. After Stalin's death he was dismissed in 1965.

3   Sir Cyril Burt dominated educational psychology in Britain up to the 1970s. He was appointed by the London County Council as the

first educational psychologist and did pioneering work in the capital to improve the education of backward children and the treatment of delinquents. In his last years he held to the theory that intelligence was largely inherited, despite accumulating evidence that the environment played a major part. Some of the evidence produced by him in this period appears to have been fraudulent.

References

AITKEN, M. A., BENNETT, S. N. and HESKETH, J. (1981) 'Teaching styles and pupil progress; a re-analysis', in *British Journal of Educational Psychology*, 51, 170–86.

ARMSTRONG, M. (1980) *Closely Observed Children*. London: Chameleon Books.

ASHTON, P. (1975) *The Aims of Primary Education*. London: Macmillan.

ATKINSON, P. (1981) 'Bernstein's structuralism', in *Educational Analysis*, 3, 1, 85–95.

AULD, R. (1976) *William Tyndale Junior and Infants Schools Public Enquiry*. London: Inner London Education Authority.

AUSUBEL, D. P. (1963) *The Psychology of Meaningful Verbal Learning*. New York: Grune and Stratton.

AUSUBEL, D. P. (1968) *Educational Psychology: a cognitive view*. New York: Holt, Rinehart and Winston.

BARKER-LUNN, J. (1970) *Streaming in the Primary School*. Windsor: NFER-Nelson.

BARNES, D. (1979) *From Communication to Curriculum*. Harmondsworth: Penguin.

BASSEY, M. (1978) *Nine Hundred Primary School Teachers*. Windsor: NFER-Nelson.

BEALING, D. (1972) 'The organisation of junior school classrooms', in *Educational Research*, 14, 231–5.

BENNETT, S. N. (1976) *Teaching Styles and Pupil Progress*. London: Open Books.

BENNETT, S. N. (1979) 'Recent research on teaching: a dream, a belief, and a model' in BENNETT, S. N. and McNAMARA, D. *Focus on Teaching*. Harlow: Longman.

BENNETT, S. N., ANDREAE, J., HEGARTY, P. and WADE, B. (1980) *Open Plan Schools: Teaching, Curriculum and Design*. Windsor: NFER-Nelson.

BENNETT, S. N., DESFORGES, C., COCKBURN, A. and WILKINSON, B. (1984) *The Quality of Pupil Learning Experiences*. Hillsdale, NJ: Erlbaum.

BERGER, P. (1961) *The Precarious View*. New York: Doubleday.

BERGER, P. and LUCKMANN, T. (1961) *The Social Construction of Reality.* Harmondsworth: Penguin.

BERNSTEIN, B. (1961) 'Social factors in educational achievement', in HALSEY, A. H., FLOUD, J. and ANDERSON, C. A. *Education, Economy and Society.* New York: Free Press, pp. 288–314.

BERNSTEIN, B. (1970) 'Education cannot compensate for society', in *New Society*, 15, 387, 344–7.

BERNSTEIN, B. (ed.) (1973) *Class, Codes and Control.* London: Routledge and Kegan Paul.

BIGGE, M. (1971) *Learning Theories for Teachers.* New York: Harper and Row.

BLOOM, B. S. (1956) *Taxonomy of Educational Objectives: Cognitive Domain.* London: Longman.

BLOOM, B. S. (1964) *Stability and Change in Human Characteristics.* New York: Wiley.

BLOOM, B. S. (1976) *Human Characteristics and School Learning.* New York: McGraw-Hill.

BLOOM, B. S. (1981) *All our Children Learning.* New York: McGraw-Hill.

BOYDELL, D. (1974) 'Teacher-pupil contact in junior classrooms', in *British Journal of Educational Psychology*, 44, 313–18.

BOYDELL, D. (1975) 'Pupil behaviour in junior classrooms', in *British Journal of Educational Research*, 45, 122–9.

BOYDELL, D. (1981) 'Classroom organization 1970–7', in SIMON, B. and WILLCOCKS, J. (eds) *Research and Practice in the Primary School Classroom.* London: Routlege and Kegan Paul.

BRANDT, R. M. (1975) 'An observational portrait of a British infant school', in SPODEK, B. and WALBERG, H. J. (eds) *Studies in Open Education.* New York: Agathon Press, pp. 101–25.

BROPHY, J. E. and EVERTSON, C. M. (1976) *Learning from Teaching.* Boston, MA: Allyn and Bacon.

BROWN, G. and DESFORGES, C. (1979) *Piaget's Theory: A psychological critique.* London: Routledge and Kegan Paul.

BURTON, D. (1983) 'I think I know that: aspects of English-language work in primary classrooms', in STUBBS, M. and HILLIER, H. *Readings on Language, Schools and Classrooms.* London: Routledge and Kegan Paul, pp. 246–62.

COHEN, D. (1983) *Piaget: Critique and reassessment.* London: Croom Helm.

COX, C.B. and DYSON, A. E. (1969) *Fight for Education: A Black Paper.* London: Critical Quarterly Society.

COX, C. B. and BOYSON, R. (1977) *Black Paper 1977.* London: Temple Smith.

DEARDEN, R. (1968) *The Philosophy of Primary Education.* London: Routledge and Kegan Paul.

DELAMONT, S. (1983) *Interaction in the Classroom.* London: Methuen.

DEPARTMENT OF EDUCATION AND SCIENCE (1967) *Children and their Primary Schools* (The Plowden Report). London:HMSO.

DEPARTMENT OF EDUCATION AND SCIENCE (1978) *Primary Education in England and Wales*. London: HMSO.

DEPARTMENT OF EDUCATION AND SCIENCE (1979) *Aspects of Secondary Education in England*. London: HMSO.

DEPARTMENT OF EDUCATION AND SCIENCE (1981) *The School Curriculum*. London: HMSO.

DEPARTMENT OF EDUCATION AND SCIENCE (1982) *Education 5 to 9*. London: HMSO.

DEWEY, J. (1916) *Democracy and Education*. New York: Macmillan.

DONALDSON, M. (1978) *Children's Minds*. London: Collins/ Fontana.

DUNKIN, M. J. and BIDDLE, B. J. (1974) *The Study of Teaching*. New York: Holt, Rinehart and Winston.

EBBINHAUS, H. (1966) *Memory: a contribution to experimental psychology*. New York: Dover.

EDWARDS, A. and FURLONG, V.J. (1978) *The Language of Teaching*. London: Heinemann.

ELASHOFF, J.D. and SNOW, R. E. (1971) *Pygmalion Reconsidered*. New York: C. A. Jones.

ENGLEMANN, S., OSBORN, J. and ENGLEMANN, T. (1972) *DISTAR Learning Program*. Chicago, IL: Science Research Associates.

FILMER, P., SILVERMAN, D. and WALSH, D. (1972) *New Directions in Sociological Theory*. London: Collier Macmillan.

GAGNÉ, R. N. (1965) *Conditions of Learning*. New York: Holt, Rinehart and Winston.

GALTON, M. and SIMON, B. (1980) *Progress and Performance in the Primary Classroom*. London: Routledge and Kegan Paul.

GALTON, M., SIMON, B. and CROLL, P. (1980) *Inside the Primary Classroom*. London: Routledge and Kegan Paul.

GALTON, M. and WILLCOCKS, J. (1983) *Moving from the Primary Classroom*. London: Routlege and Kegan Paul.

GARNER, J. and BING, M. (1973) 'Inequalities of teacher-pupil contacts', in *British Journal of Educational Psychology*, 43, 234–43.

GETZELS, J. W. (1978) 'Theoretical research and school change', in GLASER, R. (ed.) *Research and Development and School Change*. Hillsdale, NJ: Erlbaum, pp. 27–45.

HAMILTON, D. (1975) 'Handling innovation in the classroom: two Scottish examples', in REID, W. A. and WALKER, D.F. (eds) *Case Studies in Curriculum Change: Great Britain and the United States*. London: Routledge and Kegan Paul, pp. 179–207.

HARRE, R. and SECORD, P. F. (1972) *The Explanation of Social Behaviour*. Oxford: Blackwell.

HAWKINS, P. (1977) *Social Class, the Nominal Group and Verbal Strategies*. London: Routledge and Kegan Paul.

HILSUM, S. and CANE, B. S. (1971) *The Teacher's Day*. Windsor: NFER-Nelson.

INNER LONDON EDUCATION AUTHORITY (1983) *Race, Sex and Class*. London: Inner London Education Authority.

JACKSON, P.M. and BELFORD, E. (1965) 'Private affairs in public settings: observations on teaching in elementary schools', in *School Review*, Summer, 172–86.

JOYCE, B. and WEIL, M. (1980) *Models of Teaching*. New York: Prentice Hall.

KERRY, T. (1984) 'Analysing the cognitive demands made by classroom tasks in mixed-ability classes', in WRAGG, E.C. (ed.) *Classroom Teaching Skills*. London: Croom Helm.

KERRY, T. and SANDS, M. K. (1984) 'Classroom organisation and learning', in WRAGG, E.C. (ed.) *Classroom Teaching Skills*. London: Croom Helm.

KING, R. (1978) *All Things Bright and Beautiful*. Chichester: Wiley.

KOUNIN, J. S. (1970) *Discipline and Group Management in Classrooms*. New York: Holt, Rinehart and Winston.

LABOV, W. (1969) 'The logic of non-standard English', in KEDDIE, N. (ed.) *Tinker, Tailor... The Myth of Cultural Deprivation*. Harmondsworth: Penguin.

LABOV, W. (1972) *Language in the Inner City*. Philadephia, PA: University of Philadelphia Press.

LAW, D. (1977) *The Discipline and Management of Primary School Classrooms*. Unpublished MA dissertation. Lancaster: University of Lancaster.

LAWTON, D. (1975) *Class, Culture and the Curriculum*. London: Routledge and Kegan Paul.

LEITH, S. (1981) 'Project work: an enigma', in SIMON, B. and WILLCOCKS, J. *Research and Practice in the Primary Classroom*. London: Routledge and Kegan Paul.

LYNCH, A. J. (1924) *Individual Work and the Dalton Plan: The working of the Dalton Plan in an elementary school*. London: Philip.

McALEESE, R. and HAMILTON, D. (1978) *Understanding Classroom Life*. Windsor: NFER-Nelson.

MACKAY, D., THOMPSON, B. and SHAUB, P. (1970) *Breakthrough to Literacy*. Harlow: Longman.

McDOUGALL, W. (1946) *An Introduction to Social Psychology*, 28th edition. London: Methuen.

MARCUSE, H. (1964) *Eros and Civilization*. Boston, MA: Beacon Press.

NUNN, P. (1920) *Education, its Data and first Principles*. London: Arnold.

Omni (1979) May, 131–2.

PARKHURST, H. (1922) *Education in the Dalton Plan*. London: Bell.

POPPER, K. R. (1959) *The Logic of Scientific Discovery*. London: Hutchinson.

RESNICK, L. B. (1972) 'Teacher behaviour in the informal classroom', in *Journal of Curriculum Studies*, 4, 99–109.

ROGERS, C. (1951) *Client-centred Therapy*. Boston, MA: Houghton Mifflin.

ROSEN, H. and ROSEN, C. (1973) *The Language of Primary School Children*. Harmondsworth: Penguin.

ROSENTHAL, R. and JACOBSON, L. (1968) *Pygmalion in the Classroom*. New York: Holt, Rinehart and Winston.

RUTTER, M. *et al.* (1979) *Fifteen Thousand Hours*. London: Open Books.

SCHUTZ, W. (1958) *FIRO: A three-dimensional theory of interpersonal behaviour*. New York: Holt, Rinehart and Winston.

SCHUTZ, W. (1967) *Joy: Expanding human awareness*. New York: Grove Press.

SEABORNE, M. (1971) *Primary School Design*. London: Routledge and Kegan Paul.

SHARP, R. and GREEN, A. (1975) *Education and Social Control*. London: Routledge and Kegan Paul.

SHIPMAN, M. D. (1981) *The Limitations of Social Research*, 2nd edition. Harlow: Longman.

SHIPMAN, M. D. (1984) *Education as a Public Service*. London: Harper and Row.

SIMON, B. (1981) 'The Primary School Revolution: myth or reality', in SIMON, B. and WILLCOCKS, J. *Research and Practice in the Primary School Classroom*. London: Routledge and Kegan Paul.

SIMON, B. and WILLCOCKS, J. (1981) *Research and Practice in the Primary School Classroom*. London: Routledge and Kegan Paul.

SINCLAIR, J. M. and COULTHARD, R. M. (1975) *Towards an Analysis of Discourse. The English used by Teachers and Pupils*. Oxford: Oxford University Press.

SKEMP, R. (1971) *The Psychology of Learning Mathematics*. Harmondsworth: Penguin.

SKINNER, B. F. (1968) *The Technology of Teaching*. New York: Prentice-Hall.

SOUTHGATE, V., ARNOLD, H. and JOHNSON, S. (1981) *Extending Beginning Reading*. London: Heinemann.

SQUIBB, P. (1973) 'The concept of intelligence—a sociological perspective', in *Sociological Review*, 21, 1 57–75.

STIERER, B. (1982) 'Testing teachers? A critical look at the Schools Council Project, *Extending Beginning Reading*', in *Primary School Review*, 13.

STONES, E. (1979) *Psychopedagogy*. London: Methuen.

STONES, E. (1984) *Supervision in Teacher Education*. London: Methuen.

STUBBS, M. (1983) *Language, Schools and Classrooms*. London: Methuen.

STUBBS, M. and DELAMONT, S. (1976) *Explorations in Classroom Observation*. London: Wiley.

TANN, S. (1981) 'Grouping and group work', in SIMON, B. and WILLCOCKS, J. *Research and Practice in the Primary Classroom.* London: Routledge and Kegan Paul.

THOMAS, W. I. (1928) *The Child in America.* New York: Knopf.

THOMPSON, B. (1980) 'Spirit of the ant heap', in *Times Educational Supplement*, 7 November, 16–17.

WIGHT, J. and NORRIS, R. (1970) *Teaching English to West Indian Children.* Schools Council Working Paper 29. London: Methuen.

WILEY, D. E. and HARNISCHFEGER, A. (1974) 'Exploration of a myth: quantity of schooling and exposure to instruction, major educational vehicles', in *Studies of Educational Processes*, 3. Chicago, IL: University of Chicago.

WRAGG, E. C. (1978) 'A suitable case for imitation', in *Times Educational Supplement*, 15 September, 18.

WRAGG, E. C. (1984) *Classroom Teaching Skills.* London: Croom Helm.

Index